FUTURE AMERICAN SAINTS?

Future American Saints?

Men and Women Whose Causes for Canonization Are Being Considered

John F. Fink

ST PAULS

Library of Congress Cataloging-in-Publication Data

Fink, John F.
  Future American saints? : men and women whose causes for
canonization are being considered / by John F. Fink.
        p. cm.
  Includes bibliographical references. (p.   ) and index.
  ISBN 978-0-8189-1291-7
1. Catholics—United States—Biography.   I. Title.
  BX4670.F55   2008
  282.092'273—dc22
  [B]
                                   2008049932

Produced and designed in the United States of America by the
Fathers and Brothers of the Society of St. Paul,
2187 Victory Boulevard, Staten Island, New York 10314-6603
as part of their communications apostolate.

ISBN-10: 0-8189-1291-X
ISBN-13: 978-0-8189-1291-7

Printing Information:

Current Printing - first digit   1   2   3   4   5   6   7   8   9   10

Year of Current Printing - first year shown

2009 2010 2011 2012 2013 2014 2015 2016 2017 2018

DEDICATION

To Our Grandchildren:

Jacklyn

Angela

Brian

Hilary

Jack

Joseph

Hannah

Claire

Tyler

David

Erin

May you all be future saints

CONTENTS

Introduction ix

Martyrs of Virginia 1

Martyrs of Georgia 5

Eusebio Kino.. 9

Charles Nerinckx..13

Magin Catala 17

Felix De Andreis..21

Pierre Toussaint 25

Felix Varela 29

Frederic Baraga...33

Simon Bruté.. 37

Demetrius Gallitzin 40

Samuel Mazzuchelli....................................45

Henriette Delille.. 49

Mary Lange 53

Michael J. McGivney 57

Cornelia Connelly...................................... 63

Isaac Hecker 68

Mary Magdalen Bentivoglio 76

Frank Parater 81

Mary Theresa Dudzik 85

Marianne Cope... 89

Stephen Eckert 93

Nelson Baker 97

Rose Hawthorne Lathrop...........................103

James Walsh and Thomas Price 107

Marie-Clement Staub 113

Miriam Teresa Demjanovich....................... 117

Maria Luisa Josefa 121

Maria Kaupas 124

Emil Kapaun...128

Solanus Casey...131

Mary Virginia Merrick 135

Dorothy Day...138

Angeline McCrory 145

Catherine de Hueck Doherty.......................149

Fulton J. Sheen 153

Patrick Peyton...165

Walter Ciszek..177

Terence Cooke...183

Vincent Capodanno 188

Acknowledgments and Bibliography.............191

INTRODUCTION

Through the years, both in my books and in the weekly column I write for *The Criterion*, the newspaper for the Archdiocese of Indianapolis, I've written frequently about saints, hoping that their lives will inspire some readers enough to try to emulate their spiritual qualities. Among my books are *Married Saints*, two volumes about *The Doctors of the Church*, *American Saints* and *Saint Thomas More: Model for Modern Catholics*.

Alba House published my book *American Saints* in 2001. It's about those who were either canonized or beatified in all the countries of the Americas. The U.S. saints at that time were Isaac Jogues, Jean de Lalande, and Rene Goupil (the North American Jesuits who were martyred by the Mohawk Indians in what is now part of the United States; five others were martyred in what is now Canada), Elizabeth Ann Seton, Rose Philippine Duchesne, John Neumann, Frances Xavier Cabrini, and Katharine Drexel. Since then,

Mother Theodore Guerin has been canonized as Saint Theodora, but she was Blessed Mother Theodore when I wrote that book. The others who had been beatified are Kateri Tekakwitha, Junipero Serra, Francis Xavier Seelos, and Damien de Veuster.

The book you are now holding is about some other holy men and women from the United States whose causes for sainthood have been introduced. I've identified fifty-one of them in various stages of the canonization process. There won't, however, be fifty-one chapters. The martyrs of Virginia and the martyrs of Georgia will be considered together, as will Maryknoll Fathers Thomas Price and James A. Walsh.

There's no way of knowing how many of those fifty-one individuals will someday be canonized. The process of canonization is deliberately lengthy because it requires the careful study of the life of a candidate, his or her writings, eyewitness testimony if possible, and the careful study of any miracles attributed to his or her intercession. As a practical matter, it's likely that those who have lived more recently have a better chance of advancing to sainthood than those who lived in the sixteenth or seventeenth centuries. If they were going to be beatified or canonized, it probably would have happened by now.

All of those in this book have been declared either a "Servant of God" or "Venerable." "Servant of God" is the declaration by the local diocese or archdiocese that began the process that the person possessed a "reputation for sanctity" and a documented history of "heroic virtues or martyrdom." "Venerable" is the title bestowed by the Vatican's Congregation for the Causes of the Saints after it decrees that the candidate truly practiced heroic virtues. The next step is beatification, followed by canonization.

Perhaps I should say a word of explanation about why most of the chapters are quite short while others are relatively long. It's simply that we know much more about a person like Archbishop Fulton J. Sheen than we do about some of the other individuals. There's also the fact that someone like Frank Parater died when he was only twenty-two.

Some of these possible future canonized saints lived recently enough that some of my readers might have known them. I've met four of them—Father Solanus Casey, Archbishop Fulton Sheen, Father Patrick Peyton, and Cardinal Terence Cooke. Father Peyton used to visit our home when I was growing up and we prayed the family rosary with him. My personal story of Archbishop Sheen is included in the chapter about him. Others might have gotten to know Dorothy Day or Catherine de Hueck Doherty, although I never had that privilege.

I will profile these men and women in roughly chronological order, although that's difficult at times because some lived longer than others and their lives overlapped.

FUTURE AMERICAN SAINTS?

CHAPTER ONE

MARTYRS OF VIRGINIA

The North American Martyrs who were killed by the Mohawk Indians from 1642 to 1649 were canonized in 1930. But seventy-five years before Saint Isaac Jogues was killed in upper New York, eight Jesuits were martyred by Indians in what is now Virginia. They are still on the list for possible canonization.

Their story begins with the Spanish discovery of Chesapeake Bay, which Captain Angel de Villafane named the Bay of the Mother of God. Explorers returned to Spain with the usual products discovered there—fruits and vegetables—but also with an Indian boy they named Don Luis de Velasco. He was baptized and educated in Spain.

In 1570, Jesuit missionaries led by Father Juan Bautista de Segura returned to this territory, disembarking near the future site of Williamsburg. Father Segura had been the superior of a mission in Florida, but it had not been successful at converting the Indians there. He finally gave up and ordered most of his missionaries to return to their headquarters in Havana, Cuba. However, he decided to make one more attempt to convert the Indians, this time farther north.

The other missionaries were Father Luis de Quiros; Brothers Gabriel Gomez, Sancho Zeballos and Pedro Linares; and novices Gabriel de Solis, Juan Bautista Mendez and Cristobal Redondo. They brought the Indian convert Don Luis with them, since he knew the language and customs of the Powhatan Indians. In fact, his uncle was a powerful chief. They also brought along a young boy named Alonso de Olmos.

After they arrived, Don Luis set off in search of his relatives while the Jesuits built a cabin with a chapel—the first Catholic chapel in Virginia. They opened a school for Indian boys and the three novices were professed into the Society of Jesus—the first religious profession in the United States.

Father Segura became concerned when Don Luis failed to return. Soon he learned from the Indians that Don Luis had abandoned Catholicism and returned to native ways. He had married several Indian women and was living an immoral life. Father Segura sent intermediaries to persuade his convert to return, but to no avail.

On February 4, 1571 Father Quiros and novices Gabriel and Juan went in search of Don Luis. They found him and Don Luis welcomed them to his village. He listened to them and promised to follow the Jesuits back to the mission. The missionaries were to go on ahead and he would follow soon. Instead, he and several other Indians overtook the missionaries and killed them, shooting them with arrows and then beating them to death with clubs. Juan managed to escape at first, but was found the next morning and killed.

On February 9, Don Luis and fellow Indians arrived at the Jesuits' cabin. Knowing nothing about what had happened to Father Quiros and the two novices, Father Segura was overjoyed to see Don Luis after many months. He enthusiastically welcomed the Indians. The Indians offered their help and asked for axes with which to cut wood. Once they received the axes, they killed all the remaining missionaries except the boy Alonso, since it was the Indians' practice to adopt boy captives into their tribe.

Several months later, a Spanish supply ship arrived. The sailors aboard the ship became suspicious when they noticed that some of the Indians were wearing the Jesuits' cassocks. Suddenly, two boats with armed warriors appeared. A battle ensued, during which the Spanish captured two

Indians. They reported the deaths of the Jesuits and the capture of Alonso.

Eighteen months later the governor of Cuba arrived with soldiers to investigate and to rescue Alonso. He demanded Alonso's release and Don Luis's surrender. Don Luis did not surrender, but Alonso managed to escape and swim to the Spanish ship. Alonso reported the facts of the Jesuits' deaths and several Indians corroborated his story. Twelve of the Indians were tried for murdering the Jesuits. Five of them were released and seven were hanged.

The cause for these martyrs' beatification and canonization is still open and there's a postulator in Richmond, Virginia, but it seems doubtful at this late date that they will be canonized. I suspect that the French Jesuits made more of an effort to get the North American Martyrs canonized than the Spanish Jesuits did for the Virginia martyrs.

CHAPTER TWO

MARTYRS OF GEORGIA

In the previous chapter I wrote about the Jesuit martyrs who were killed by Powhatan Indians in Virginia in 1571. Twenty-six years later, in 1597, Guale Indians killed missionaries in the coastal area of Georgia. This time the missionaries were Franciscans. Their fifty-mile mission stretched from Saint Catherine's Island in the north to the Cumberland Islands in the south. Father Pedro de Corpa, who had arrived as a missionary in 1587, was the regional superior. Father Blas de Rodriguez, who had arrived in 1590, lived at the mission.

The Indians' rampage began after the two priests decreed that the Indian Juanillo should not be permitted to succeed his uncle as chief. Juanillo had married two women and the priests decided between them that the practice of bigamy would undermine the faith in the mission. The priests appointed an elderly Indian named Francisco. This enraged Juanillo. He left the village and organized opponents of the new religion.

One night the Indians sneaked into the village of Tolomato where, at daybreak, they found Father Corpa praying quietly at the Mission Nuestra Señora de Guadalupe. They tomahawked him, decapitated him and put his head on a spear at the canoe landing area. Juanillo gave a speech, saying, "He would not have been killed had he let us live as we did before we became Christians. Let us return to our ancient customs." The Indians then proceeded to rape the Christian women and generally looted the mission.

From Tolomato, the Indians went to Mission Santa Clara at Tupiqui, where they told Father Rodriguez that they had come to kill him. He asked if he could say Mass before he died and the Indians permitted him to do so. They also allowed him to live for two more days.

During that time, he told them, "My sons, for me it is not difficult to die. Even if you should not cause it, the death of this body is inevitable. All of us have to die some day. But what does pain me is that the evil one has persuaded you to do this offensive thing against your God and creator."

The Indians tomahawked him to death on September 16 and threw his body where dogs might eat it. But faithful Indians recovered the body and buried it.

There were two missionaries at Saint Catherine's Island. The chief there warned them that Juanillo was on the warpath and even offered a canoe to escape. For whatever reason, they refused. When the Indians arrived, they first killed Brother Antonio, then Father Miguel de Anon.

Father de Verascola had gone to Saint Augustine, Florida, for supplies, unaware of what was happening. When he returned, the Indians went to the shore as if to welcome him, but then sprang on him. He was a strong man, known by his brother missionaries as "the giant from Cantabria," but the Indians overpowered him, bound him and put him in an animal's cage. After three days they tried to burn him to death, but a heavy rainstorm prevented it. Eventually they hacked him to death with an axe.

Father Francisco de Avila was still left. He learned what was happening and hid in the forest by his mission, now Jekyl Island. He was captured and the Indians decided to keep him as a slave, which they did for nine months. Since the Indians did not kill him, he is not included among the martyrs of Georgia.

The Spanish governor at Saint Augustine

sent soldiers to find the rebels. Juanillo was caught and killed. Father Avila was rescued and returned to Saint Augustine where he wrote down the events as he knew them. He refused, however, to testify against the Indians at a trial because he didn't want anyone to die as a result of his testimony.

By 1605, nine years after the massacre, the Franciscan missions were operating again.

CHAPTER THREE

EUSEBIO KINO

Both the United States and Mexico can legitimately claim Jesuit Father Eusebio Francisco Kino. His statue is in Statuary Hall in the U.S. Capitol for the state of Arizona, although he did much of his work in the Mexican state of Sonora. His cause for beatification and canonization has been open for a long time, probably too long for it to happen, but he's still on the list.

He wasn't Spanish as you'd expect from his name, but rather an Austrian from the Italian Tyrol. His original name was Kuhn, with Kino being the Spanish equivalent. After becoming a member of the Jesuit's German province, he distinguished himself in the study of mathematics, cartography and astronomy. He taught mathematics at the University of Ingolstadt. However, he wanted to be a missionary in Asia like his model, Saint Francis Xavier. He got his wish to be a missionary, but he was sent to North America instead of Asia.

He arrived in Mexico in 1681 and taught in Mexico City for a while. One of the things he did while teaching there was to show his expertise as an astronomer by publishing a book about his observations of a comet.

In 1683 he went to Baja California where he served in a mission there for two years. At that time, scholars taught that Baja California was an island. Through extensive research, Father Kino was the first to establish that it actually is a peninsula.

When the mission in Baja California was closed in 1685, he returned to Mexico City. Then, from 1687 until his death twenty-four years later, he worked in the vast territories in northern Sonora in Mexico and southern Arizona, New Mexico and California. During that time he founded scores of towns and cities.

Professor Herbert Bolton of the University of California called him "the most picturesque missionary pioneer of all North America—explorer, astronomer, cartographer, mission builder, ranchman, cattle king, and defender of the frontier."

He is credited with more than fifty expeditions as he and his comrades explored the country between the Magdalena and Gila rivers and the Colorado River to the Gulf of California. No one has ever calculated the thousands of miles he must have traveled on horseback. He traveled thirty to forty miles a day, including halts to preach and baptize. He is credited with baptizing four thousand five hundred Pima Indians. He opened trails that are roads today. He kept careful journals of his travels and observations, and his papers are preserved in the Huntington Library in San Marino, California.

Father Kino's maps were the most accurate of the time. One of the maps he produced in 1705 covered an area two hundred miles east-to-west and two hundred fifty miles north-to-south. His maps and several books he wrote brought him fame in Europe.

He also began nineteen cattle ranches in southern Arizona and northern Mexico. He introduced European grains and fruits. Wheat culture in California began with a handful of seed he sent across the desert to a Yuma chief who had once befriended him. A mission he began in 1698 was famed for its fields of wheat, herds of cattle, sheep and goats.

He built the original Church of San Xavier del Bac outside of Tucson, a popular tourist stop today. However, he did not build the elaborate church that stands there now. It was built between 1783 and 1797 by Franciscans. It still serves Indians in the area.

Father Kino died at age sixty-six while on one of his travels. He rode out from his mission in Dolores, northern Mexico, to dedicate a chapel. He became ill during his Mass and died there on March 15, 1711 with calfskin as a mattress and his pack saddle for a pillow.

He was surely one of the greatest missionaries this country has ever known. He preceded by some eighty-two years Franciscan Father Junipero Serra, the founder of the California missions who was beatified by Pope John Paul II in 1988.

CHAPTER FOUR

CHARLES NERINCKX

Before coming to the United States and moving to Kentucky in 1804, Father Charles Nerinckx was a priest in Belgium. He had served as an assistant at the cathedral for eight years and was pastor of a church in Everberg-Meerbeke for eleven years.

It was a tough time, though, to be a priest. This was in the years immediately following the French Revolution when the Catholic Church was still being persecuted. In 1797 the Belgian government required all priests to take an oath of hatred against royalty and Father Nerinckx refused to do so. For seven years he hid during the day in the attic or chicken coop of a hospital administered by his aunt, a Benedictine nun. At night he visited Catholics, instructing them and hearing confessions. His two a.m. Masses sometimes attracted as many as two hundred people.

By 1803, after narrowly escaping from soldiers who tried to arrest him, Father Nerinckx decided that it would be best for him to leave Belgium. A friend who was a wealthy nobleman wrote to Bishop John Carroll in Baltimore about Father Nerinckx and Bishop Carroll immediately replied with a letter inviting the priest to come to America. When he was forty-three, Father Nerinckx escaped from Belgium by walking for ten days to Amsterdam, where he boarded a ship for the United States. After three months in what he described as "a floating hell," he disembarked in Baltimore in November of 1804. He studied English for four months at Georgetown University and then lived with Bishop Carroll for a month before Bishop Carroll assigned him to the Kentucky Territory.

His pastoral area was a square, two hundred miles from north to south and from east to west—about half of the state of Kentucky. He visited his flock on horseback, taking six weeks to make a circuit, constantly adding communities and building churches. In 1815 and again in 1820 he traveled back to Europe in search of priests and money for his mission. One of his recruits was Father Peter De Smet, who was to become one of the greatest missionaries to the American Indians. During both of his trips he also returned with numerous crucifixes, chalices, paintings and other religious articles, many of which are displayed in the chancery of the Archdiocese of Louisville or at the motherhouse of the Sisters of Loretto.

He founded the Sisters of Loretto, known formally as the Friends of Mary at the Foot of the Cross, in 1812. It was the first community of religious women founded in the United States. Their mission was mainly to teach girls, especially the poor, slaves and Indians. During the twelve years between their founding and Father Nerinckx's death, the community grew to more than a hundred members. It continues today and its motherhouse and novitiate are in the small town of Nerinx, Kentucky.

In 1808, John Carroll, by then the Archbishop of Baltimore, recommended that Father Nerinckx be appointed Bishop of New Orleans. When the appointment came, though, Father Nerinckx declined it because he thought he had too much to do in Kentucky.

In 1824, though, he asked Bishop Benedict Flaget, Bishop of Bardstown, to permit him to move farther west. Apparently the bishop had received complaints from other priests about Father Nerinckx's alleged excessive rigor and austerity. Bishop Joseph Rosati of New Orleans accepted him and assigned him to the Upper Louisiana Territory, now Missouri. Father Nerinckx hoped to develop missions among the Indians there.

He left Loretto on June 16, 1824. But less than two months later he died at St. Genevieve, Missouri. His body was transported back to the sisters' motherhouse at Loretto ten years later.

CHAPTER FIVE

MAGIN CATALA

Franciscan Father Magin Catala's life sounds similar to that of Franciscan Father Junipero Serra's. Father Magin served in the missions founded by Father Junipero, who is now known as Blessed Junipero. Father Magin arrived in California nine years after Father Junipero's death.

Both men were originally from Spain and both entered the Franciscan seminary when they were sixteen. (Magin had a twin brother who entered the seminary with him.) Both Father Junipero and Father Magin volunteered to labor in the New World missions and both were sent to the College of San Fernando in Mexico City, Father Junipero arriving there in 1750 and Father Magin in 1786. Father Junipero went on to California where he founded nine missions before his death in 1784. Eventually there would be twenty-one missions.

After studying Indian languages and mission methodologies in Mexico City, Father Magin was sent to Monterrey in 1793. His first assignment was as chaplain on a Spanish ship that sailed regularly between Mexico and Vancouver, then known as Nootka Sound. After a year of this, the governor asked him to continue but he declined because he wanted to devote his life to the Indians in California.

After a short time at Mission San Francisco, in 1794 Father Magin moved forty miles south to Santa Clara, the eighth of Father Junipero's missions. He remained assigned to that mission until his death thirty-six years later, ministering to more than a thousand Indians who lived there.

Although he was assigned to the Santa Clara mission, that doesn't mean that he stayed there all the time. Father Magin knew that there were thousands more Indians in the villages, so he traveled extensively as far as the San Jacinto Valley, about a hundred miles away, seeking unconverted Indians. A prayer card said of him, "Often he made perilous journeys to distant tribes and invariably returned accompanied by large numbers of pagan Indians whom his sweet charity had induced to abandon their wild life for the happy Christian community at Santa Clara."

He walked to the Indian villages despite

extremely painful rheumatism that he contracted early in his work. In this, too, he resembled Father Junipero, who was severely crippled from an infected foot, except that Father Junipero rode on a mule.

Another priest arrived several years after Father Magin, so that priest was assigned responsibility for overseeing the material well-being of the mission while Father Magin concentrated on the Indians' spiritual well-being. He instructed them in the Catholic faith and taught such devotions as the Stations of the Cross and the Rosary. He preached from a pulpit until his rheumatism got too bad for him to climb it. From then on, he preached while sitting in a chair by the altar rail. He built new churches for the mission, first in 1818 and again in 1825.

According to a biographer, Father Magin baptized five thousand four hundred seventy-one infants, children or adults, presided at one thousand ninety-five weddings and more then five thousand funerals.

He was known for his asceticism and sanctity. He ate very little and no meat, eggs or wine. His evening meal consisted only of gruel made from corn and milk. He practiced disciplines popular in those days. He prayed long hours before a life-size crucifix in the chapel, and was sometimes seen to be levitating. Those who testified to his sanctity attributed miracles, prophecies, revelations and locutions to him.

He died in 1830 at age sixty-nine.

CHAPTER SIX

FELIX DE ANDREIS

Felix De Andreis, born in 1778 in northern Italy, joined the Vincentians (formally, Congregation of the Mission) that Saint Vincent de Paul founded in 1625, and was ordained a priest in 1802. He spent the first four years of his priesthood preaching parish missions in northern Italy. When he began to have health problems, his superiors transferred him to Rome where he taught seminarians for ten years while continuing to give missions and preach retreats for both priests and laity.

While Father De Andreis was preaching one of his retreats for priests, Bishop Louis DuBourg of Louisiana heard him and was impressed. The bishop was in Europe recruiting priests. He asked Father De Andreis if he was interesting in going to the New World and perhaps starting a seminary there. Father De Andreis immediately answered enthusiastically. His Vincentian superior, though, didn't want to let him go because he was already involved in the education and formation of priests. The superior was also concerned that Father De Andreis wasn't healthy enough for the missions in the New World since he had already had health problems in northern Italy. Bishop DuBourg was determined to get Father De Andreis, so he took the matter directly to the pope, who assigned two cardinals to decide the case. They sided with Bishop DuBourg and Father De Andreis was permitted to go.

First, however, Bishop DuBourg, Father De Andreis and the Vincentian superior signed a contract that stipulated that Father De Andreis would have to recruit five or more Vincentians to go with him, that they would live a common life and maintain the Vincentian style of missions in the New World, and that the bishop would erect a seminary for them.

Father De Andreis recruited thirteen volunteers—priests, brothers and seminarians. The first recruit was Father Joseph Rosati, whom Father De Andreis had taught in the seminary. He was later to become Bishop of St. Louis and administrator of New Orleans.

The recruits left Italy in two groups and met in Bordeaux, where they planned to study French in preparation for going to New Orleans. While they were studying, though, a letter arrived from Bishop DuBourg changing their assignment to St. Louis. So they studied English during their six-week voyage from Bordeaux to Baltimore. Not just English, though. Father De Andreis turned the ship into a sailing seminary, maintaining a schedule that included daily Mass, the Liturgy of the Hours, spiritual reading, and theology classes.

After arriving in Baltimore, their next stop was Bardstown, Kentucky. They went overland from Baltimore to Pittsburgh, then down the Ohio River to Louisville, and then thirty miles to St. Thomas Seminary in Bardstown. Father De Andreis stayed there a year, teaching theology and studying English.

In 1817, he went to St. Louis with Father Rosati and Bishop Benedict Flaget of Bardstown. A journey that began in Rome in October of 1815 finally ended in St. Louis in October of 1817. Almost immediately, Bishop DuBourg named Father De Andreis vicar general of Upper Louisiana. While filling those duties he erected a seminary at Perryville, Missouri, and began the first novitiate of the Vincentians in the United States.

He also somehow found time to evangelize African-Americans, both slave and free, and the Indians. He learned the local Indian dialect enough to translate the Our Father. He planned to write a catechism in the Indian language, but he ran out of time.

The Vincentian superior was right in questioning whether Father De Andreis's health was sufficiently good for the missions. In more than thirty-five letters, Father De Andreis described the hardships he experienced and his continual illnesses. His stomach ailments continued to worsen and he died only four years after he arrived in the United States, on October 15, 1820 at age forty-two.

He has been declared Venerable but has never been beatified.

CHAPTER SEVEN

PIERRE TOUSSAINT

Venerable Pierre Toussaint, a former slave, is the only layman to be buried among cardinals and archbishops in St. Patrick's Cathedral in New York. When he died in 1853 at age eighty-seven, no other place seemed as appropriate for a man regarded as a saint.

If he is ever canonized he could become the patron saint of hairdressers because that's what he did for a living. (Hairdressers already have Saints Martin de Porres and Mary Magdalene as patron saints.)

Toussaint was born in 1766 as a slave in Haiti (then known as Saint Dominique) on a plantation owned by the Frenchman Jean Jacques Berard. Since Toussaint worked as a domestic servant, he learned to read and write, and play the violin.

In 1791 Berard foresaw that Haiti's slaves, who comprised four hundred fifty thousand of the five hundred twenty thousand population, were about to revolt. Berard thought it best to leave the country. He took his family, two sisters-in-law and five domestic slaves, including Toussaint and his sister Rosalie, to New York. The slaves in Haiti did revolt in a bloody rebellion and won their freedom in 1793.

In 1801, Berard returned to Haiti to see if anything was left of his plantation. There wasn't. He wrote a letter to his wife Marie saying that everything they owned was "irretrievably lost." Soon Marie received another letter: Jean Jacques had contracted pleurisy and died.

When the Berards had moved to New York ten years earlier, Toussaint had become apprenticed to a hairdresser. He soon became popular with the wealthiest women in New York, who were generous when paying for Toussaint's services. With his income, he was able to support Madame Berard and the household until Madame Berard contracted tuberculosis and died in 1807, when she was only thirty-two. She and Toussaint had arranged that he would be released from slavery when she died. He also inherited the Berard home where he lived before eventually purchasing another home.

In 1811, when he was forty-five, Toussaint married another former slave from Haiti, Juliette Gaston. Unable to have children, they adopted the six-month-old daughter of his sister Rosalie, whose husband had abandoned his family. The child, Euphemia, died from tuberculosis when she was fourteen.

Toussaint continued his work as a hairdresser and his business thrived. Customers appreciated his work but also his obvious closeness to God. They often sought his advice. He quoted the Beatitudes, *The Imitation of Christ*, and the French writer Father Jacques Bossuet. He would explain devotion to the Blessed Mother and other teachings of the Catholic Church, quoting from some of the Church's great spiritual writers. If any gossip should happen to occur in his shop, he would say in broken English, "Toussaint dresses hair; he no news journal." His customers got the point.

Toussaint attended Mass and said the Rosary daily in St. Peter's Church, which then was the only Catholic church in New York. He helped Elizabeth Ann Seton raise funds for orphans and, after she founded the Daughters of Charity, he helped support that community. When he discovered that the New York City orphanage would not accept black children, he opened an orphanage for them in his own home. He also began the first school for black children in the city when it was illegal to educate Negroes. He provided food, clothing and shelter to black refugees from Haiti while quietly also aiding some of the French who had lost their fortunes in Haiti. When about half of New York City's population fled the city during a yellow fever epidemic, he remained behind to nurse victims, including bringing a white man with yellow fever into his home.

After forty years of marriage, Juliette died in 1851 and Pierre Toussaint buried her beside their daughter Euphemia. Two lonely years later, Pierre also died.

CHAPTER EIGHT

FELIX VARELA

Felix Francisco José Maria de la Concepçión Varela y Morales was well known in his native Cuba before he fled for his life in 1823.

He was born in 1788 in Havana. His parents both died by the time he was six, so he was raised by his grandparents and other relatives. He always knew that he wanted to be a priest, so he entered the seminary when he was fourteen and was ordained when he was only twenty-three.

As a priest he earned degrees in philosophy, theology, chemistry and civil law. He taught in the seminary in Cuba while editing several journals and publishing a number of books, one of them a three-volume course in philosophy. By the time he was thirty-three, in 1821, he was recognized as Cuba's foremost thinker and writer. He taught his students to love God, his people, and Cuba.

In 1821 he was appointed to represent Cuba

at the Court of the Constitutional Monarchy in Madrid, Spain. When the appointment came, his first reaction was to reject it, but he was obedient to his bishop who encouraged him to accept the appointment. At the court, he advocated the abolition of slavery, racial equality, equal education for boys and girls, constitutional government for all Spanish colonies, and reform of Spain's criminal laws.

In 1823, though, the Absolute Monarchy returned to power in Cuba and executed more than a thousand reformers. Father Varela quickly fled for his life, taking a ship for New York City. At first New York's Bishop John DuBois hesitated about accepting this reformer, but, after making an investigation with Church leaders in Cuba, welcomed him to the diocese.

After assignments to two other parishes, the cathedral, and then Christ Church, in 1832 the bishop appointed Father Varela the founding pastor of the Church of the Transfiguration of Our Lord, where he served for twenty-five years. His parish was composed of immigrants—Irish, Poles, Germans, Austrians, Swiss, French, Spanish and Cubans.

As he had done in Cuba, he wrote. Now it was articles for several English and Spanish periodicals. He revised his course in philosophy and wrote a catechism for the diocese. He also began a diocesan newspaper and founded the first Spanish newspaper in the United States. He brought parish missions to the diocese. He served as theologian to both Bishop DuBois and his successor, Archbishop John Hughes, and eventually became vicar general of the archdiocese.

But he did far more. He established an orphanage staffed by the Sisters of Charity. He advocated for public assistance for Catholic school children. He became a hero in the city during a cholera epidemic in 1832 because of his care for the victims. He won approval of having Catholic chaplains in the city's hospitals and charitable institutions. He formed alliances with the city's scientists, including André Parmentier, the founder of the Brooklyn Botanic Garden. He organized the New York Catholic Temperance Association for those addicted to alcohol.

During an era of severe anti-Catholicism Father Varela courageously defended the Catholic Church through his published articles. He also wrote about human rights, cooperation between English- and Spanish-speaking communities, and the importance of education. Through it all, he continued to work tirelessly for Cuba's political independence from Spain.

Father Varela was worn out by his early sixties and suffered from illnesses. He became less active and eventually moved to St. Augustine, Florida, where he died in 1853 at age sixty-five. His body was taken back to Cuba and buried in the Great Hall of the University of Havana.

In 1997, the U.S. Post Office issued a commemorative stamp in Father Varela's name and image for his extraordinary contributions.

CHAPTER NINE

FREDERIC BARAGA

F rederic Baraga was another missionary to
the American Indians, this time to the
Chippewas and Ottawas.

He was born in Slovenia in 1797 and was
ordained a priest in 1823. At that time the emperor
was a believer in Jansenism, a heresy named after
Cornelius Jansen that denied the free will in accepting or rejecting God's grace. The heresy had
originally been condemned by Pope Innocent X
in 1653, but it popped up again in the eighteenth
century and was condemned again by Pope Pius
VI in 1794. Father Baraga, therefore, was a vehe-
ment opponent of Jansenism—but his bishop was
not. The bishop transferred Father Baraga to a
remote parish in the diocese.

In 1830, Father Baraga learned that the
Leopardine Foundation was searching for missionaries to send to North America. He applied
and was accepted by Bishop Edward Fenwick of

Cincinnati. Father Baraga sailed to New York and then traveled west to meet his new bishop.

Cincinnati was still a diocese rather than an archdiocese then, but it covered a lot of territory. Bishop Fenwick assigned Father Baraga to the northwest part of the diocese, eighty thousand square miles that included Michigan's Upper Peninsula and parts of Minnesota and Wisconsin. There he ministered to occasional fur traders and miners, but his principal parishioners were Chippewa and Ottawa Indians. He established missions in Indian villages throughout the vast area. He traveled to his missions by foot, horseback or canoe most of the year, but in the winter it was by snowshoes. In a letter to his bishop he wrote:

> In winter a person cannot travel otherwise than on foot. As the snow is generally deep and there are no traveled roads, the only way to travel is on snowshoes. These snowshoes are from four to five feet long and one foot wide and are tied to one's feet. With them a man can travel even in the deepest snow without sinking in very much. But this style of walking is very tiresome, especially for Europeans, who are not accustomed to it.

He also had to sleep in forests or out in the open because, as he wrote, "A man may travel four or five days in this extensive and thinly settled country before coming to another Indian settlement." He wrote that an Indian guide who accompanied him "sleeps the whole night as if he were in a featherbed."

Baraga was named first Bishop of Sault St. Marie, Michigan, in 1853. The diocese was relocated to Marquette in 1866 because of its more central location.

Bishop Baraga spoke and wrote Slovenian, French, German, English and Chippewa. After becoming bishop he wrote his first pastoral letter in Chippewa. He was a prolific writer, so he couldn't have been traveling all the time. He wrote seven prayerbooks in Slovenian and twenty books in English on religious topics as well as a sociological description of the Indian tribes he knew. He also wrote a dictionary and grammar of the Chippewa language, plus a catechism and hymnal. His diaries totaled three volumes.

He was also known for his sanctity. He rose each morning at four a.m. to spend three hours in prayer.

Besides ministering to the Indians, Bishop Baraga was also their champion, objecting to government authorities about the policy of removing the Indians from their native lands and selling alcohol to them. He prayed for justice for the Indians as well as peace among them.

Bishop Baraga traveled to and attended the Council of Baltimore in 1866. While there he suffered a stroke. He asked the priest who accompanied him to take him back to his wilderness diocese so he could die there. He lived another sixteen months before his death in 1868.

CHAPTER TEN

SIMON BRUTÉ

We sometimes forget that the French made great contributions to the Catholic Church in the United States. In 1817, every Catholic bishop in the United States except one had been born in France. Many priests who had been forced out of France at the time of the French Revolution came to the United States.

Vincennes was the first diocese in Indiana, established in 1834, and its first four bishops were born in France. Its territory included all of Indiana plus the eastern part of Illinois. Simon William Gabriel Bruté de Remur was appointed the first bishop.

Bruté was born in Rennes, France in 1779. As he grew up he was educated for the medical profession, but then he decided to become a priest. He was ordained in 1808 and two years later came to the United States. He was a seminary professor at St. Mary's Seminary in Baltimore for most of his life, until his appointment to the wilderness of Indiana when he was fifty-five years old.

At the time of his appointment, Bruté owned one of the largest collections of books in the United States. He had about five thousand volumes transported all the way from Baltimore to Vincennes. He added them to the library that Bishop Benedict Flaget began forty years earlier when he was a priest in Vincennes. It was the largest library west of the Allegheny Mountains.

Bishop Bruté lost no time in trying to solve the personnel and money problems of his new diocese. In 1835 he traveled back to France on a begging mission. At his hometown of Rennes he recruited Benjamin Petit. He ordained him in 1837 and sent him to serve the Potawatomi Indians in northern Indiana. The young priest went with the Indians when they were forcibly moved to Kansas, and he died in 1839.

While in France, too, Bishop Bruté met with the seminarians at the newly formed Congregation of Holy Cross. Edward Sorin was one of those seminarians and he was captivated by Bishop Bruté's apostolic zeal and his accounts of ministering to Indians and white families in the Indiana wilderness. After his ordination Father Sorin led a group of Holy Cross brothers to Indiana and he founded the University of Notre Dame in 1842.

By that time, though, Bishop Bruté was dead.

While in France, Bishop Bruté also asked church officials for a priest who could act as his assistant and eventually succeed him as bishop. Father Celestine de la Hailandiere was selected, and he became vicar general of the Diocese of Vincennes.

In 1838, Bishop Bruté sent Father de la Hailandiere back to France, this time to find a congregation of nuns willing to establish a mission in the diocese. He met with the Sisters of Providence, who traveled to Indiana under the leadership of Mother Theodore Guerin, who has been canonized as Saint Theodora. (I devoted a chapter to her in my book *American Saints*.)

Bishop Bruté died on June 26, 1839, after only five years as the first bishop of Vincennes. But he made a good beginning.

CHAPTER ELEVEN

DEMETRIUS GALLITZIN

While Simon Bruté was serving as the first bishop of Vincennes from 1834 to 1839, another priest had already become prominent in western Pennsylvania. He was one of the more interesting priests in the early history of the Catholic Church in America.

Demetrius Augustine Gallitzin was a Lithuanian prince. Tall, dark and handsome, he was born in The Hague in 1770 while his father was Russian ambassador to Holland. His father's family was known in Russian history as "the Great Galitsyns." His mother was part of the German nobility, daughter of Field Marshal von Schmettau, commander of Frederick the Great's army.

Demetrius was raised for a military career and became a skilled horseman and swordsman. When he was ten, he was sent to Munster, Germany, where he received his formal education. He learned to speak three languages and he played at least three musical instruments. However, his father scoffed at religion and Demetrius was raised in a pagan atmosphere.

When Demetrius was sixteen, his mother became seriously ill. Afraid that she was about to die, she asked for a priest and, against her husband's will, returned to the Catholic faith into which she had been born. She recovered from the illness and from then on prayed to Saint Monica that Demetrius, too, would turn to religion. He did and, after studying various religions, became convinced that the Catholic faith was the true one. He converted to Catholicism when he was seventeen.

He continued his military career and, by age twenty-two, was aide-de-camp to an Austrian general in Austria's war against the French. But then all foreigners were suddenly dismissed from the Austrian Army. Demetrius decided to go to America where he thought the new nation could use trained soldiers. He assumed the name Augustine Smith when he left Europe so as not to call attention to his aristocratic status. He arrived in the United States in 1792.

Once here, though, he changed his mind about a military career, partly because of the influence of his travel companion, a Catholic priest named Felix Brosius. Feeling called to the priesthood, Demetrius offered his services to Bishop John Carroll, Bishop of Baltimore. The bishop was glad to have him. Gallitzin attended the new St. Mary's Seminary in Baltimore and Bishop Carroll ordained him to the priesthood on March 18, 1795. He was the second priest to be ordained in the United States and the first to receive his training here. (Father Stephen Badin, missionary to Kentucky, was the first to be ordained, but he studied in Europe.)

After ordination, Father Smith, as he continued to call himself, worked with three other priests in Virginia and Maryland while also celebrating Mass for the German-speaking Catholics in Baltimore. On one occasion, he was asked to attend to a Protestant woman who wanted to convert to Catholicism on her deathbed. He went, even though the woman lived about one hundred thirty miles west of Baltimore. The experience convinced him that a priest was needed in that area. Therefore, when he returned to Baltimore, he asked Bishop Carroll to transfer him there.

In 1799, the bishop assigned him to the frontier in western Pennsylvania. There, for forty-one years, he was almost constantly on horseback as he ministered to Catholics over an area that included the present dioceses of Pittsburgh, Greensburg, Altoona-Johnstown, Harrisburg and Erie.

Using his own money, Father Smith started the town of Loretto as a Catholic establishment. He used the town as his base while he traveled to serve the people within about a hundred-mile radius. He built a log church in 1800 and doubled its size in 1808, finally replacing it with a larger church in 1818. By the time of his death, the town of Loretto included ten churches and three monasteries serving about five thousand Catholic families. Still using his own money, he built an orphanage, a grist mill, a saw mill, and a tannery for the people. It has been estimated that he spent one hundred fifty thousand dollars of his inheritance (as valued in 1800 dollars).

When not traveling to visit his flock, he wrote pamphlets defending Catholicism and evangelizing: *Defense of Catholic Principles* in 1816, *An Appeal to the Protestant People* in 1819, *A Letter to a Protestant Friend on the Holy Scriptures* in 1820, and *The Bible: Truth and Charity* in 1836.

The Diocese of Baltimore became an archdiocese in 1808 and Loretto became part of the Diocese of Philadelphia. He became vicar general for Western Pennsylvania in 1823. He was asked to become the first bishop of Pittsburgh, but he refused and Pittsburgh didn't become a diocese until three years after his death. At various times he was asked to become bishop of the dioceses of Cincinnati, Detroit, Philadelphia, Bardstown, and for some sees in Germany, all of which he declined.

Father Gallitzin continued to call himself Father Augustine Smith until after his father's death, when he assumed his true identity.

In 1834, when he was sixty-four, Father Gallitzin was thrown from his horse and seriously injured a leg. That injury and the normal effects of aging slowed him down, but the prince-priest who became a pioneer-priest continued to work for six more years until his death on May 6, 1840.

CHAPTER TWELVE

SAMUEL MAZZUCHELLI

You might know about a young man named Matthew Kelly, a speaker and author who is able to excite his audiences when he speaks about Catholicism. But there was a much earlier man whom the Irish settlers in the Upper Peninsula of Michigan called Matthew Kelly. His real name, though, was Father Samuel Mazzuchelli. Even his bishop, Mathias Loras, called the priest Matthew Kelly.

The life of Samuel Mazzuchelli seems similar to that of Frederick Baraga, about whom I wrote in Chapter Ten. Like Father Baraga, Father Mazzuchelli answered the call for missionaries in the Diocese of Cincinnati, which then included the current states of Ohio, Indiana, Illinois, Michigan and Wisconsin.

He was born in Milan, Italy in 1806, the youngest son of a wealthy banker. His mother died when he was six. Against his father's wishes, he joined the Dominican Order in Rome when he was seventeen and began his studies for the priesthood. While he was still a seminarian, Bishop Edward Fenwick, also a Dominican, sent his vicar general to Europe to recruit priests. Mazzuchelli was interested, so he requested and received permission to go to the United States.

He left Rome, went to Milan to say goodbye to his family, sailed from La Havre to New York, and west to Cincinnati. He completed his theological studies in Somerset, Ohio, and Bishop Fenwick ordained him a priest in 1830. The bishop sent him to Mackinac Island, eight hundred miles north of Cincinnati. He was the first priest to minister in Michigan's Upper Peninsula in sixty years, from the time the Jesuits had to leave the region when the Society of Jesus was suppressed in 1773. Father Baraga joined him there about a year later.

He worked among the Menominee, Winnebago and Chippewa Indians as well as French-Canadian fur traders. Like Father Baraga, he traveled all over the vast territory on foot, horseback, canoe and snowshoes. He founded numerous parishes and built three churches, including the first church in Wisconsin, in Green Bay in 1830-31. In 1833 he published a prayerbook for the Winnebago Indians and the next year he published a liturgical calendar in the Chippewa language.

As more priests arrived in Michigan, Father Mazzuchelli moved southwest to the region where Wisconsin, Illinois and Iowa meet, and there he remained from 1835 until his death. He made his principal residence in Sinsinawa, Wisconsin. He is credited with founding about thirty parishes and building fourteen churches. He founded St. Thomas Aquinas College and St. Clara Academy. The college closed after his death. The academy became Dominican University at River Forest, Illinois.

This area had a population boom when lead was discovered, growing from about eighteen thousand people to seventy thousand in the seven-year span from 1838 to 1845. The Diocese of Dubuque was founded in 1837, with Mathias Loras (the one who called Father Mazzuchelli "Matthew Kelly") as its first bishop. The bishop appointed "Father Matthew Kelly" vicar general.

Father Mazzuchelli suffered a severe illness in 1843, when he was thirty-seven. He returned to Milan, Italy, where his family still lived, for a year. While there he wrote his *Memoirs* to acquaint Italians with his work in the United States and to recruit other missionaries.

Before his return to America in 1844, the Dominican Order appointed him a Missionary

Apostolic, giving him authority "to establish the Dominican Order on the banks of the Upper Mississippi." With that authority, he established a novitiate and Sinsinawa Mound College as a school for boys. Both, however, proved to be unsuccessful and ceased to exist. He was more successful when he founded the sisters' community of Sinsinawa Dominicans of the Most Holy Rosary. It continues to exist, but he transferred it to Benton, Wisconsin, where he served as pastor the last fifteen years of his life.

Besides building churches, Father Mazzuchelli also designed civic buildings, including the state capitol in Iowa City, the courthouses in Galena, Illinois, and Fort Madison, Iowa, and the Market House in Galena.

Throughout his ministry, Father Mazzuchelli was an advocate for the Indians, writing on their behalf to the governor, president and members of the U.S. Congress.

He contracted pneumonia on February 23, 1864 after traveling on a bitterly cold morning to anoint two parishioners. He died that evening at age fifty-seven.

CHAPTER THIRTEEN

HENRIETTE DELILLE

Henriette Delille is the first U.S.-born African American whose cause for canonization has officially been undertaken. She was born in New Orleans in 1812 and was known at the time as "a free woman of color."

Her great-great grandmother had been brought from Africa as a slave. Claude Dubruiel, a French colonialist, bought her and had her baptized as Marie Ann in 1745. Although he was married to a white woman, Claude and Marie had four children. One of Claude's legitimate children freed his half-siblings after Claude's death.

Naturally, the Catholic Church condemned it, but the practice of white married men having black mistresses was a tolerated institution in New Orleans society in those days, even among Catholics who otherwise practiced their faith. The law prohibited free women of color from marrying white men and there were few free men of color, so what was known as the quadroon system flourished. A "quadroon" is a person of one-quarter black ancestry. As she matured, white men propositioned Henriette as part of the system and her sister Cecile had four children with a white man, but Henriette refused to have anything to do with the quadroon system.

She was only seventeen when she gathered three other free women of color and they began to catechize African-Americans, both slave and free, in the basics of the Catholic faith. After seven years of that, they formed a pious confraternity called the Congregation of the Sisters of the Presentation of the Blessed Virgin Mary.

At first they didn't live in community but took vows of poverty, chastity and obedience and dedicated their lives to helping African-Americans and persons of color. Their rule said that each sister was to "seek to bring back the Glory of God and the salvation of their neighbor by a charitable and edifying behavior," working together since "each woman alone could do little to evangelize or care for others." They were to work for the sick, the infirm, and the poor.

In 1842, though, the women began to live in community, in a house bought for them by the cathedral's pastor. The community affiliated with the international Sodality of the Blessed Virgin

Mary. In their book *Henriette Delille: "Servant of Slaves,"* Virginia Meacham Gould and Charles E. Nolan wrote, "It was during the existence of slavery, in the year 1842, that this humble Institution was founded. Four young ladies, natives of this city, and descendants of some of our most respectable families of color (free), burning with zeal for the salvation of souls, commenced by teaching catechism and preparing colored girls and women for their First Communion."

The number of sisters grew and Henriette formed the Association of the Holy Family, whose members helped support the congregation with money and prayers. In 1850 she purchased a home where the sisters conducted religious instruction for children during the day and for women at night.

The sisters lived simply and in great poverty. Gould and Nolan wrote, "Many were the times that the foundresses had nothing to eat but cold hominy that had been left from some rich family's table." They described their clothing as "more like Joseph's coat that was of many pieces and colors, darned until darn was not the word."

In 1852, Henriette and some of the other sisters traveled to Convent, Louisiana, north of New Orleans, where Archbishop Antoine Blanc arranged for them to receive formal instruction in religious life from the Religious of the Sacred Heart. They stayed there for several months.

Henriette died when she was only fifty, in 1862 during the Civil War. Seven years later the Vatican gave formal recognition to the religious community.

CHAPTER FOURTEEN

MARY LANGE

Elizabeth Clarisse Lange was a refugee from the revolution in Saint Dominique (now known as Haiti), around 1812, when she was twenty-eight. She went to Baltimore, then a haven for those who escaped Haiti's revolution and those who escaped from the French Revolution. Both groups spoke French.

This was, of course, a time when blacks in the South didn't enjoy the same rights as whites. It was, for example, illegal to educate black children. Elizabeth did so anyway. Beginning around 1818, she and a friend, Marie Balas, also a refugee from Haiti, turned Elizabeth's home into a school for black girls.

The Haitian refugees in Baltimore were being helped by the Sulpician Fathers. They had been forced to leave France during the French Revolution. Those who immigrated to the United States were welcomed by Bishop John Carroll.

They founded St. Mary's Seminary in Baltimore in 1791, the first seminary in this country. Since both the Sulpicians and the Haitians spoke French and were Catholics, the Sulpicians allowed the Haitian community the use of a basement chapel in the seminary.

They also assigned Father Jacques Joubert to pastor the Haitian refugees. His family had escaped the French Revolution by moving to Saint Dominique. When revolution occurred there, too, he alone of his family made it to the United States in 1804. He entered St. Mary's Seminary and was ordained a priest. It seemed natural that he would be appointed to pastor the Haitians.

In 1828, when Elizabeth had been teaching black girls for ten years, Father Joubert suggested to her that they start a religious community of black women with the mission of educating black women. Elizabeth agreed. She and three other Haitian women became the founders of the Oblate Sisters of Providence. Elizabeth took the religious name of Mary, Marie Balas became Sister Mary Frances, Rosanne Boegue became Sister Mary Rose, and Almaide Duchemin became Sister Mary Theresa. After the other women elected Elizabeth as the first superior, she was called Mother Mary the rest of her life.

With the help of the four women, Father

Joubert wrote the Constitution and Rules for the new community. Archbishop James Whitfield approved them in 1829 and Pope Gregory XVI did so in 1831, making the Oblate Sisters of Providence the first community of religious women of African descent.

The following years, though, were difficult as the sisters suffered from prejudice. Maria M. Lannon wrote in her book *Response to Love: The Story of Mother Mary Elizabeth Lange, O.S.P.*, "The sisters had to endure verbal insults, along with threats of physical abuse from some of Baltimore's white Catholics who objected to colored women wearing the habit of a nun."

The sisters suffered from extreme poverty, surviving on the small amounts paid by parents of their students and from the sale of needlework, sewing, mending and working as laundresses at St. Mary's Seminary and Loyola College.

Even ecclesiastical superiors refused to help. After Archbishop Whitfield, no other archbishop during Mother Mary's lifetime supported the community, one of them suggesting that the sisters disband and return to the lay state. However, they did have some supporters. After Father Joubert died in 1843, the Redemptorist Fathers became chaplains to the sisters in 1847. Father Thaddeus Anwander went door-to-door begging contributions for the sisters, and seeking students for the school. Redemptorist Father John Neumann, who would later become Archbishop of Philadelphia and a canonized saint, traveled to Baltimore four times a year to serve as the sisters' confessor.

Despite the difficulties, the community continued to add members and schools. The sisters opened schools in Fells Point, Maryland; Philadelphia, New Orleans, and another in Baltimore. However, they all closed for financial reasons.

In 1860 the Jesuits bought a house for the sisters if the sisters would do the laundry at Loyola College. In 1879, the Josephite Fathers became chaplains for the sisters.

Mother Mary was superior for nine years, although not all consecutively. After the first three years, in 1832 she asked not to be re-elected. But in both 1835 and 1838 she allowed herself to be nominated for superior, and each time she was elected.

As she aged, she remained in her room at St. Francis Academy in Baltimore except for Mass, but enjoyed visits from her sisters and students. She died there, after receiving Communion, on February 3, 1882. She was ninety-eight.

CHAPTER FIFTEEN

MICHAEL J. McGIVNEY

Father Michael McGivney was ordained only four years in 1882 when he founded the Knights of Columbus. He did it out of pastoral concern for the welfare of his parishioners, most of whom were poor Irish immigrants.

Like so many other Irish, both of Michael's parents fled Ireland because of the potato famine in the 1840s. They were married in Waterbury, Connecticut, in 1850. Michael was the eldest of their thirteen children, six of whom died in infancy. He was a bright child, so much so that when it came time for him to start school he skipped the first two grades. In those days, students typically graduated from high school when they were sixteen, but Michael finished school when he was thirteen. Although he expressed a desire to be a priest, his father opposed the idea and Michael went to work in a brass factory for three years.

His father finally relented when Michael was

sixteen and allowed him to study for the priest-hood. He attended the College of Saint-Hyacinthe in Quebec, Canada, the Seminary of Our Lady of Angels at Niagara University, and then Sainte-Marie College in Montreal. While he was there, his father died. Michael packed his bags and returned to Waterbury, certain that he would have to find a job to help support his family and knowing that his family could no longer support him in the seminary.

However, word soon came to Bishop Francis McFarland that one of the most promising men in the diocese needed financial help. He gave Michael the equivalent of a full scholarship and sent him to St. Mary's Seminary in Baltimore, where he finished his studies. Archbishop (later Cardinal) James Gibbons ordained him on December 22, 1877 in Baltimore's Cathedral of the Assumption.

His first assignment was St. Mary's Church in New Haven, Connecticut, where he quickly got to know his parishioners through visits to the sick and other priestly responsibilities. One of the things he learned was how quickly families could become destitute if the husband and father died in those days before Social Security. Discrimination against Catholics, especially the Irish, was widespread in the late 1800s. When they were able to find jobs, an injury or death could leave their families penniless and homeless.

Father McGivney envisioned an insurance and benevolent society that would care for such families. After discussing his idea with his bishop and learning about benevolent societies in Boston and Brooklyn, he gathered the men of his parish together. After months of discussion about insurance, minimum and maximum ages for membership, initiation fees, and the disbursement of benefits, they founded the Knights of Columbus in May of 1882, with the first council at St. Mary's Church in New Haven. Father McGivney became its secretary.

It had a slow start. Father McGivney tried to get other parishes to join, but without initial success. Soon the members began to complain and suggested that they should give up and disband. Father McGivney did his best to hold the organization together. He prepared a clear statement of its purpose, structure and conduct for the Supreme Knight, the Supreme Council, the Supreme Committee, the Supreme Chaplain, and the Knights themselves.

Finally he began to see some progress. In 1883 five other parishes in Connecticut expressed an interest in joining. That increased to twelve by the end of 1884. At the society's second convention, in 1884, Father McGivney stepped down as secretary and accepted the role of Supreme Chaplain.

The Knights benefited when Pope Leo XIII, in 1884, published an encyclical that condemned Freemasonry and encouraged Church leaders to form Catholic societies to combat secret societies such as the Masons. The *Connecticut Catholic* editorialized that the Knights of Columbus "is eminently fitted" to "ward off the dangers of those secret societies" which were proscribed by the Church.

By the end of 1885 there were thirty-one councils. By that time, though, Father McGivney had been transferred to St. Thomas Church in Thomaston, a poor parish in an impoverished factory town. He again threw himself wholeheartedly into serving both the spiritual and physical needs of his parishioners while continuing his role in the Knights of Columbus. The organization continued to expand, reaching a membership of five thousand in fifty-one councils in 1889.

Then, in 1890, Father McGivney contracted pneumonia, which evolved into tuberculosis. This was not particularly surprising. As Douglas Brinkley and Julie M. Fenster wrote in their book *Parish Priest: Father Michael McGivney and American Catholicism,*

In the 1880s, parish priests did not generally live very long, under any circumstances. From 1874 to 1886, the Hartford Diocese counted about eighty-three priests at any one time. Yet during that same span seventy diocesan priests died. That translates to a turnover of almost eighty-five percent in a dozen years. Going into the priesthood, young men knew that they had little chance of reaching fifty years of age and almost no hope of reaching seventy.

The priests were overworked, and their short life span led to even more work for those who were left.

Father McGivney died on August 14 of that year, two days after his thirty-eighth birthday. His funeral Mass, naturally celebrated by his bishop, attracted seventy of his brother priests and over two hundred fifty members of the Knights of Columbus in addition to hundreds of parishioners from both St. Thomas in Thomaston and St. Mary's in New Haven.

By 2006 the Knights of Columbus had a million seven hundred thousand members in thirteen countries. It had more than a million five hundred thousand premium-based insurance policies in effect. It had become one of the largest charitable organizations, in 2004 alone making contributions totaling one hundred thirty-five million dollars.

CHAPTER SIXTEEN

CORNELIA CONNELLY

Venerable Cornelia Connelly had several things in common with Saint Elizabeth Ann Seton. Both were converts, wives, mothers who suffered the loss of children, and founders of religious orders. But the circumstances surrounding Cornelia's founding an order were considerably different from Elizabeth Ann Seton's.

Born Cornelia Peacock in 1809 in Philadelphia, she was the youngest of nine children, including two step-sisters from her mother's first marriage. After her parents died, she was adopted by one of her step-sisters, Isabella Bowen Montgomery. The family went to the Presbyterian Church, but when she was twenty-two, Cornelia switched to the Episcopal Church.

That same year she married Pierce Connelly, vice-rector of an Episcopalian church, who was twenty-seven. In 1832, he became rector of an

Episcopalian church in Natchez, Mississippi, and they moved there. Their first two children, Mercer and Adeline, were born there.

During a period of anti-Catholicism, Pierce studied the accuracy of accusations against the Catholic Church and its history. This resulted in his conversion to Catholicism. Cornelia, too, received instructions in Catholicism and became a Catholic two months before Pierce did.

Pierce, though, not only became a Catholic, he also wanted to become a priest. He traveled to Rome to see how that could be arranged. Pope Gregory XVI suggested that he take his time in making such a decision since he was a new convert and the decision would mean that he could no longer be married to Cornelia.

Pierce and Cornelia moved to Grand Coteau, Louisiana, where Pierce taught at the Jesuit College of St. Charles and Cornelia gave private piano and guitar lessons. They had two more children while in Grand Coteau, but their fourth child died when seven months old. Three months later two-year-old John was killed in a horrible accident when a large dog knocked him into a sugar cane boiler, scalding him. He died two days later.

Cornelia was pregnant with their fifth child when Pierce asked her if she would be willing to live a celibate life so he could become a priest.

Cornelia very reluctantly agreed and Pierce left to study in Rome, taking their eldest child, eight-year-old Mercer, with him. He enrolled Mercer in a boarding school in London and then proceeded to travel around Europe, making no attempt to keep in touch with Cornelia, who was back in Grand Coteau with their other two children.

Pierce again went to Rome and spoke again to Pope Gregory XVI about becoming a priest. The pope refused to make a decision until after he had spoken with Cornelia, so Pierce returned to Louisiana, gathered Cornelia and the children, and took them to Rome. The pope encouraged Pierce to spend time with Cornelia and their children, but he agreed to permit Pierce to be ordained a priest if Cornelia took a vow of perpetual chastity. Feeling that she had little choice, she did so on June 18, 1845. Three days later Pierce was ordained a priest.

Now what was Cornelia to do? At the suggestion of her spiritual adviser, Jesuit Father John Grassi, she founded the Society of the Holy Child Jesus. The archbishop of Westminster, England, asked her and three other women to staff a new Catholic school in Derby. The children were put in boarding schools.

Mother Cornelia (all the sisters were called mothers) arrived in Derby in 1846. The school served the English poor and Irish immigrants who had fled the potato famine. The sisters had little money but they taught children during the day and their mothers at night. Under Cornelia's leadership, the sisters taught the liberal arts and science but also included music, dance, art, and drama. The night school for the children's mothers attracted a hundred women. Also, during the first two years, twenty-one postulants joined the society.

Then, suddenly, Pierce showed up at the convent's door in March of 1847. He had changed his mind about being a Catholic priest and demanded that Cornelia return to their married state. She refused and insisted that he leave the convent at once. He became enraged and in January of 1848 kidnapped their children from their boarding schools. At that time, in England, the courts considered a man's wife and children as his property.

After six months, Pierce again appeared at the convent, behaving as if nothing had happened. Cornelia refused to talk with him until he released their daughter to her. She then went to her room and prayed, while Pierce cried in the convent's parlor. He finally left, but a year later he sued in the court of the Church of England for restoration of his conjugal rights. He won! Naturally, Cornelia appealed, but it took another two-and-a-half years before she won the appeal. She lost her children but did not have to return to married life with Pierce. Pierce eventually, but not until 1868, became rector of the American Episcopal Church in Florence, Italy. He died in 1883.

Cornelia's and Pierce's eldest child, Mercer, died in a yellow fever epidemic in New Orleans in 1852. Adeline stayed with her father until he died and seldom saw her mother. At first alienated from the Catholic Church, she returned later in life, after discussions with one of the Sisters of the Holy Child Jesus. Frank, who became a successful artist, remained alienated from the Church, blaming the Church for ruining his family.

Cornelia spent the rest of her life with the Sisters of the Holy Child Jesus. When she died in 1879 at age seventy, the society had grown to one hundred fifty-five sisters in seven houses in England, France and the United States. In Philadelphia, the sisters operate Rosemont College, my wife's *alma mater.*

CHAPTER SEVENTEEN

ISAAC HECKER

Isaac Thomas Hecker, one of the most important American Catholics in the nineteenth century, was born on December 18, 1819. He grew up to have a deep yearning for a faith that would satisfy his intellectual curiosity. Around the year 1841, he met Orestes A. Brownson, who was to have a great influence on him.

When he was twenty-three, Hecker went to live at Brook Farm, a community dedicated to a search for a better way of life. Such men as Nathaniel Hawthorne, George Bradford, Ralph Waldo Emerson, and Henry Thoreau took part in discussions there. However, Hecker was unable to find in this man-made Utopia what he was looking for.

By this time Orestes Brownson was preaching and writing Catholic doctrine, although he himself had not yet received the gift of faith.

Hecker too studied the Catholic religion and at length decided that he should enter the Church. He was conditionally baptized in old St. Patrick's Cathedral by Bishop John McCloskey (later to become America's first cardinal) on August 2, 1844. Brownson was baptized less than a year later.

Hecker then felt a call to religious life. He entered the Redemptorist novitiate in 1845, when he was twenty-six. After ordination to the priesthood, he conducted parish missions along with other Redemptorists for twelve years.

At this time, German was the language spoken in all Redemptorist houses. The Americans among the Redemptorist mission band, however, felt it would be wise to establish a new house either in New York or in Newark, New Jersey that could serve as headquarters for the English-speaking Redemptorists. So in May 1857 the Redemptorists in New York wrote to the rector major of the order, a Father Mauron, presenting the plan to him.

Father Mauron's reply was disappointing. He opposed any separation within the congregation. Again Father Walworth, the superior of the English-speaking group, wrote to the rector major explaining that English was the language of America and that the work of the missions was being damaged by the fact that Americans considered the Redemptorists established only for the German-speaking Catholics.

By now it was generally felt that one of the Americans would have to go to Rome to present the whole matter to the rector major in person. Father Hecker was chosen and he sailed for Rome, arriving on August 26, 1857. On August 30 there was a meeting of the general council of the congregation, and Father Hecker was called to the meeting. Expecting to present his case to the council, he was stunned when the rector major declared that it had been decided not to hear him. Furthermore, his coming to Rome constituted an act of disobedience. He was told that he was released from his vows and dismissed from the congregation.

Naturally believing himself to be wronged, Father Hecker appealed his case directly to the Holy See. He won the sympathy of several cardinals and eventually Pope Pius IX himself took a personal interest in the matter. Father Hecker had an audience with Pope Pius on December 17, 1857.

While awaiting a decision by the pope, Father Hecker wrote two articles for *Civiltà Cattolica*, a leading journal in Rome. These two articles showed his thoughts about the Church in the United States and how devoted he was to his country. He wrote that the principles of government in the United States were decidedly in favor of the interest and success of the Catholic religion. He suggested that Divine Providence had prepared the American people for conversion, and that it only remained to take advantage of the situation.

He concluded his first article by declaring that an abundant harvest was ready in America because many people with "an unsatisfied active intelligence and an active mind" were ready to receive the truths of the Catholic religion.

The second article dealt with the character of political institutions in the United States and their effects on the religious development of the nation. Hecker quoted the "no establishment" clause of the Constitution that leaves all religious matters to the churches rather than to the state and forbade the state to interfere with religious beliefs. Therefore, Hecker wrote, the government of the United States and its natural advantages offer a wide door to the Catholic religion.

Hecker wrote that it was necessary only to appeal to the intelligence of many outside the Church to convince them of the truth. He said that this would be a new campaign for the Church. He predicted that some day the Catholic Church might even look for missionaries from the United States to convert the Japanese and the Chinese.

On March 6, 1858, the pope dispensed Father Hecker and his four American companions from their vows as Redemptorists, and authorized them to form a new congregation devoted to missionary work in the United States. That order, the Congregation of the Missionary Priests of St. Paul the Apostle (the Paulists) is the only religious community founded solely with the purpose of providing missionary work to the United States. It is strictly an American congregation, founded in America, by Americans, for Americans, and on American principles. Its mission is nothing less than the conversion of the United States to Catholicism.

Father Hecker lived for thirty years after the founding of the Paulists. He devoted himself during that time to building up his community and finding new methods for explaining the Catholic Church to Americans. He recognized the power of the printed word and in 1865 founded *The Catholic World*, a monthly magazine that served the Church well for more than a century. He also began the Catholic Publication Society to publish pamphlets and books. This exists today as the Paulist Press, one of the largest Catholic publishers in the United Sates.

In 1870, Baltimore's Archbishop Martin Spalding selected Father Hecker to attend the Vatican Council as the archbishop's theologian. At the council, Hecker met two American bishops who were to be decisively affected by him— Bishop James Gibbons of North Carolina (later Cardinal Gibbons, Archbishop of Baltimore) and Archbishop John Ireland of St. Paul.

Although he was anxious to resume his work when he returned to the United States, his health began to fail. He was in ill health the rest of his life and practically an invalid for his last five years. Nevertheless, he continued his writing in *The Catholic World* and in 1887 a collection of his more important essays was published in a book, *The Church and the Age.* He died in 1888 at age sixty-nine.

Nine years later, in 1897, Father Hecker was indirectly responsible for a heresy that went under the name of "Americanism"—a heresy that had to be condemned by the pope. Abbe Felix Klein, a professor at the Catholic Institute of France who greatly admired Father Hecker, translated into French the book *The Life of Father Isaac Thomas Hecker*, written in 1891 by Paulist Father Walter Elliott, with an introduction by Archbishop Ireland. With the translation, Abbe Klein wrote a glowing, if somewhat inaccurate, preface to the book. He praised Father Hecker as the ideal type of modern priest who could overcome Protestantism with new methods.

The French royalists immediately condemned the book as preaching heresy. They said that Father Hecker's method of winning converts was to water down doctrine to such an extent that Father Hecker was really a Protestant. Suddenly American bishops learned that French clergymen were condemning something called Americanism. They were dumfounded. To them Americanism meant nothing more than love of country and they couldn't imagine what the fuss was all about in France. Both Cardinal Gibbons and Archbishop Ireland protested vehemently.

Archbishop Ireland decided to go to Rome to defend the Church in America. However, he arrived in Rome too late, because five days before his arrival Pope Leo XIII felt compelled to act. On January 22, 1899 he signed an encyclical addressed to "Our Beloved Son, James Cardinal Gibbons." This encyclical, *Testem Benevolentiae* ("Proof of Our Love"), condemned tendencies "which some comprise under the name of Americanism."

The pope's encyclical specifically mentioned some teachings found in the French edition of *The Life of Father Hecker*, such as over-reliance on the

Holy Ghost's individual guidance; the stressing of "natural" over "supernatural" virtues; the distinction between "active and passive" virtues; and the use of "new" methods of winning converts. But he also was careful to proclaim that he was not condemning the American spirit and that Americanism was not necessarily a doctrine accepted by Americans. He retained the name, he wrote, because it was so used in Europe.

Father Hecker, this great American priest, would be completely exonerated if the Church decides to canonize him.

CHAPTER EIGHTEEN

MARY MAGDALEN BENTIVOGLIO

The life of Venerable Mary Magdalen Bentivoglio was one of perseverance in a land where, at the time, the vocation of contemplative nuns wasn't appreciated.

Born in Italy in 1834 and baptized Annetta Bentivoglio, she was the twelfth of sixteen children. She followed her older sister Constanza into the Poor Clares of the Urbanist Rule and took the religious name Mary Magdalen of the Sacred Heart of Jesus. (Constanza didn't change her name.) After ten years they asked to be transferred to the stricter Poor Clare Sisters of the Primitive Observance of San Damiano.

In 1875 both women were selected to establish a cloister in the United States. Pope Pius IX requested the order's expansion to the United States, the Franciscan minister general supported the idea, and a Franciscan order in Minnesota requested their presence. Before they left, Sister

Mary Magdalen was named abbess and from then on was known as Mother Magdalen.

When they arrived in New York, though, they received a message that the Franciscans in Minnesota were expecting teaching sisters, not cloistered nuns. Mother Magdalen went to see Cardinal John McCloskey of New York, who wasn't interested in having contemplative sisters, telling them that "their form of life was contrary to the spirit of the country." They tried Philadelphia, where Archbishop James Wood initially welcomed them. Two months later, though, influenced by Cardinal McCloskey, he withdrew his approval, telling the sisters that a contemplative order was contrary to the apostolic direction of the United States.

They moved on to Cincinnati, but were rejected there, too, this time by Archbishop John Purcell. As Franciscan Father Pius J. Barth wrote in a chapter about Mother Magdalen in Joseph Tylenda's book *Portraits in American Sanctity*, the bishops in those dioceses "sought to recruit these cultured ladies as teachers, nurses, social workers, and catechists, but these ministries were not part of the vocation of a Poor Clare."

Finally, Archbishop Napoleon Perche of New Orleans invited the sisters there. They arrived in March 1877 and their first postulant joined them.

But then the Franciscan provincial who had been delegated authority over Mother Magdalen arrived and ordered the sisters to leave New Orleans because they were too far from other Franciscan houses. He suggested Cleveland, so the three sisters moved there in August 1877. Their convent was a converted cigar factory.

In January 1878, Carmelite Sisters from the Netherlands joined them. But the two communities didn't mix well. They spoke different languages and the sisters from the Netherlands followed a more relaxed rule. After five months Mother Magdalen led the other two Poor Clares back to New Orleans because she knew that people there wanted them. However, shortly after they got back to New Orleans, the vicar apostolic of Omaha, James O'Connor, invited them to Omaha, where the Creighton family offered them a home. Then that home was destroyed by a tornado in 1878! Construction of a new monastery wasn't finished until 1882. After trying to found their community in four cities in seven years, the sisters were finally able to do so. Soon postulants were admitted and sisters from an active religious community transferred to join them.

As the community began to grow in Omaha, Mother Magdalen inadvertently got on the wrong side of Bishop O'Connor. A second community of Poor Clares of the Primitive Observance was begun in New Orleans and the Franciscan minister general asked Mother Magdalen to travel to New Orleans to advise the new community. When Bishop O'Connor learned of her absence from Omaha, he felt insulted that she had neglected to tell him that she would be gone. Mother Magdalen apologized to the bishop, and he forgave her.

In 1888, though, Mother Magdalen and Sister Constanza were denounced by an emotionally unstable sister. She accused them of irregular personal conduct, alcoholic intemperance, financial mismanagement, and acting without due deference to the bishop. Bishop O'Connor believed the accusations and asked for a formal canonical investigation. When the investigation found no substance to the accusations, Bishop O'Connor insisted on another investigation—with the same result.

Bishop O'Connor then wrote to Bishop Richard Gilmour of Cleveland, asking for his opinion of the Poor Clares. Bishop Gilmour replied that, in his opinion, "There is no place in the American Church for drones and non-workers such as the Poor Clares." So Bishop O'Connor called a third investigation in February of 1889. For the third time, the investigation found no substance to the accusations. Nevertheless, Bishop O'Connor ordered a formal interdict upon the sisters' monastery. There were to be no Masses, no Communion, no Eucharist reserved, and no postulants accepted.

At this point, the Vatican intervened. Three priests showed up and asked Mother Magdalen and Sister Constanza to leave the convent while they investigated the accusations. For two weeks they stayed with the Sisters of Mercy while the investigation proceeded. On the final day of the investigation, the sisters who had made the accusations failed to show up. They had left town. The priests dropped all charges and in January of 1890 the Vatican sent a letter to Bishop O'Connor exonerating the Bentivoglio sisters.

Mother Magdalen established another Poor Clares community in Evansville, Indiana, the Monastery of St. Clare. Mother Magdalen led three other sisters there. It was a difficult time, the sisters literally living for a time on bread and water.

In 1902 Sister Constanza died. Three years later, Mother Magdalen became deathly ill. Aware that she was about to die, she asked the sisters to allow her to lie on a mat on the floor in imitation of the way Saint Francis of Assisi died. She then asked the sisters to stop praying for her recovery. She died in 1905 at age seventy-one.

CHAPTER NINETEEN

FRANK PARATER

The Diocese of Richmond, Virginia, introduced the cause for sainthood of Frank Parater, mainly because of a "last will" he left "to be opened only in the case of my death." He was a twenty-two-year-old seminarian at North American College in Rome when he died of rheumatic fever on February 7, 1920.

He dated his will December 5, 1919 when he was in perfect health but apparently with a strong prescience that he would die soon. He had begun studies at the seminary only ten days earlier, on November 25.

A classmate discovered his will and took it to the rector. It was translated and published in *L'Osservatore Romano*, the Vatican newspaper. Pope Benedict XV requested a copy, as did his successor, Pope Pius XI.

In his will, Parater mentioned three saints who also died young: John Berchmans, at twenty-

two; Aloysius Gonzaga, at twenty-three; and
Stanislaus Kostka, at eighteen.

Here is most of what he wrote:

I have nothing to leave or give but my
life, and this I have consecrated to the
Sacred Heart to be used as he wills. I
have offered my all for the conversions
to God of non-Catholics in Virginia.
This is what I live for and, in case of
death, what I die for.

Death is not unpleasant to me, but
the most beautiful and welcome event
of my life. Death is the messenger of
God come to tell us that our novitiate
is ended and to welcome us to the real
life.

Melancholic or morbid sentimental-
ity is not the cause of my writing this,
for I love life here, the college, the men,
and Rome itself. But I have desired
to die and be buried with the saints.
I dare not ask God to take me lest I
should be ungrateful or be trying to
shirk the higher responsibilities of life;
but I shall never have less to answer
for—perhaps never to be better ready
to meet my Maker, my God, my All.

Since I was a child, I have desired to die for the love of God and for my fellow man. Whether or not I shall receive that favor I know not.

I have always desired to be only a little child, that I may enter the Kingdom of God. In the general resurrection I wish to always be a boy and to be permitted to accompany Saints John Berchmans, Aloysius and Stanislaus as their servant and friend. Do we serve God and man less worthily by our prayers in heaven than by our actions on earth? Surely it is not selfish to desire to be with him who has loved us so well.

I shall not leave my dear ones. I will always be near them and be able to help them more than I can here below. I shall be of more service to my diocese in heaven than I could ever be on earth.

If it is God's will, I will join him on Good Friday, 1920, and never leave him more—but not my will, Father, but thine be done!

Frank Parater grew up in Richmond, attended both a Catholic elementary and high school, and then Belmont Abbey College Seminary near Charlotte, North Carolina. His bishop considered him a promising candidate for the priesthood so he sent him to North American College. He made a positive impression there on both the faculty and his fellow seminarians; the latter selected him as master of ceremonies for the celebration of the feast of the Epiphany, January 6.

He began to feel the rheumatic pains that would kill him on January 22. Doctors began to treat him for rheumatic fever, but his condition continued to deteriorate and he was placed on the critical list on February 5. He received the sacraments of penance and the anointing of the sick. On February 7 he tried to get out of bed to receive Communion, but could not; he knelt on his bed to receive. He died that morning.

The seminary's rector asked one of Frank's classmates to gather up his belongings. It was then that the "last will" was discovered. When it was read to the other seminarians, there was rejoicing because they had had a saint in their midst.

CHAPTER TWENTY

MARY THERESA DUDZIK

Josephine Dudzik was born in Kamien, Poland, about a hundred seventy-five miles from Warsaw, in 1860, the third of six children. From her earliest days she constantly searched for ways to help those in need.

As thousands of other Polish families did, the family began to emigrate from Poland to Chicago in the 1870s. First her two oldest sisters moved there in 1873 and began to prepare the way for their mother and the four other children, who arrived in 1881 when Josephine was twenty-one. The family settled in Chicago's northwest side, in St. Stanislaus Kostka Parish, which served as the center of religious and community life for the immigrant Polish community.

Resurrectionist Father Vincent Barzynski had become pastor of the church in 1874, three years after the Great Chicago Fire. With the influx of so many Polish families, the parish grew within twelve years from four hundred families to eight thousand families—forty thousand people—with a school for three thousand students, a convent for forty teaching sisters, and meeting rooms for fifty-one societies. It became the largest parish in the United States at the time.

Upon her arrival, Josephine became aware of the city's poor, sick and homeless who were living in crowded and unsanitary conditions. She began to bring many of these people into the apartment she shared with her mother. Father Barzynski became her spiritual director and he referred needy people to her. Soon he came to depend upon her to solve problems the people brought to him. Parishioners elected Josephine to leadership positions in the parish's societies. She worked as a seamstress to make enough money to feed herself, her mother, and the people she brought into their home.

Josephine later wrote in her journal, "Once while at prayer, a thought suddenly occurred to me to rent or purchase a home in the vicinity of St. Stanislaus Kostka Church and assemble all the [Franciscan] tertiaries from this parish who would desire to join me in a common life of prayer, labor, and service."

With the help of another Polish woman, Rosalie Wysinski, Josephine did exactly that in 1893 and established the community that became the

Franciscan Sisters of Chicago. Father Barzynski encouraged the two women and, knowing of their devotion to the Blessed Virgin, suggested that they place the new community under her patronage. The women did so and the order was formally founded on the feast of the Immaculate Conception, December 8, 1894. Five other Franciscan tertiaries joined. It was the first order of nuns founded in Chicago and the first Polish religious community in the United States.

Josephine, who now called herself Sister Mary Theresa, was unanimously elected superior. The community at first lived in her apartment but soon moved to larger quarters. The sisters sewed and did laundry to support themselves and the penniless residents they took in. Then, on the advice of Father Barzynski, they moved to Avondale, a fast developing area five miles northwest of Chicago.

Things did not always go well with the new community. The seven original women, in their thirties and forties and accustomed to their independence, didn't always get along. Within three years, four of them had left. There was also friction with Father Barzynski, who at times reprimanded Sister Mary Theresa and he once reversed a decision she had made concerning one of the sisters.

In 1897 the community obtained a loan to build St. Joseph Home for the Aged and Crippled. Father Barzynski signed the document since unmarried women, especially women religious, could not secure loans.

In 1898, when St. Joseph Home opened, Father Barzynski suddenly removed Sister Mary Theresa as superior of the order. She wrote that she felt "as if a heavy stone had fallen from around my neck, and I perceived unusual happiness." She remained, however, administrator of St. Joseph Home.

A year later the sisters expanded the mission of St. Joseph Home to accept the care of the children of St. Vincent Orphanage Asylum.

Sister Theresa was diagnosed with cancer early in 1918 and died on September 20, 1918 at age fifty-eight. At the time of her death the community she founded had grown to one hundred twenty-five sisters who were serving at St. Joseph Home, St. Vincent Orphan Asylum, three day care centers, and thirty-one elementary schools in seven states. Today their motherhouse is in Lemont, Illinois.

CHAPTER TWENTY-ONE

MARIANNE COPE

Father Damien de Veuster, the "leper priest" of Molokai, Hawaii, is one of our American saints. He was beatified in 1995 and Pope Benedict XVI canonized him on April 26, 2009. I included a chapter about him in my book *American Saints* since Hawaii is now a U.S. state and his statue is in Statuary Hall in the U.S. capitol in Washington. He went to the leper colony on Molokai in 1873.

Ten years later, Venerable Marianne Cope answered the plea for a community of nuns to nurse the sick poor in Hawaii, especially the lepers on Molokai. She was then forty-five years old and the provincial of the Third Order of St. Francis in Syracuse, New York. She was to spend thirty-five years serving the victims of Hansen's disease in Hawaii.

Mother Marianne was born Barbara Cope in Heidelberg, Germany. Her family came to the

United States when she was one and settled in Utica, New York. When she was fifteen she felt called to religious life, but the wages she was earning in a factory were needed by her family. However, a month after her father died in 1862, when she was twenty-four, she entered the Third Order of St. Francis, a religious community founded by Bishop John Neumann, one of our American saints. She taught in elementary schools in northern New York for eight years. As a member of the governing board of her community, she was involved in the decision to open hospitals in Utica and Syracuse. Then she was appointed chief administrator of St. Joseph's Hospital in Syracuse. Seven years later she was elected provincial.

After Father Damien established his mission among the lepers, a priest representing the vicar apostolic of Hawaii sent letters to over fifty religious congregations, including Mother Marianne's, seeking sisters to work on Molokai. Mother Marianne was the only one who replied, but she did so enthusiastically, saying, "My interest is awakened and I feel an irresistible force drawing me to follow this call."

The priest traveled to Syracuse to meet with Mother Marianne and her sisters. When he described the needs of the lepers on Molokai, Mother Marianne became even more enthusiastic. She convinced the Father Provincial of the Franciscan community to allow six sisters to go to Hawaii. The plan was for Mother Marianne to accompany them to Hawaii to establish the new ministry, but then to return to Syracuse to continue her work as provincial. They arrived in Hawaii in November of 1883.

Once in Hawaii, though, it became apparent that Mother Marianne was needed there. There was considerable work to be done to establish the sisters there, obtain governmental approval for their plans, and being present to implement them. She wrote back to Syracuse that she simply had to remain in Hawaii for an extended period of time. Then, when Father Damien contracted terminal leprosy in 1884, there was no possibility that Mother Marianne would return to Syracuse.

The sisters began their work at Kakaako Branch Hospital, where two hundred patients were crowded in rooms built to house one hundred. By 1888, Mother Marianne had opened three facilities: a general hospital on Maui, the Kapiolani Home for healthy girls of leprous parents on Oahu, and the C. R. Bishop Home for homeless women and girls with leprosy on the Kalaupapa peninsula at Molokai. In 1888 the Hawaiian Board of Health required all lepers to be transferred to Molokai. Mother Marianne moved there but continued to care for her sisters' spiritual needs in other parts of Hawaii. The sisters on Oahu continued to care for the children at Kapiolani Home.

Father Damien died in 1889 and Mother Marianne began to care for his boys as well as for her girls, as she had promised Father Damien she would do. She always insisted on strict sanitary procedures and no sister ever contracted the highly contagious Hansen's disease.

She had to worry about more than the health of the lepers. It was dangerous for women lepers and she insisted that the women on Molokai be protected from groups of drunken men who attacked those who had no police to guard them. There were also predators who awaited the girls and boys as they arrived in the settlement.

In 1902 Mother Marianne wrote to her nephew, Paul Cope, "I am working for God, and do so cheerfully. How many graces did he not shower down on me, from my birth till now?"

She died at Kalaupapa on Molokai in 1918 when she was eighty.

CHAPTER TWENTY-TWO

STEPHEN ECKERT

Capuchin Father Stephen Eckert was known primarily for his service in the African-American community during the first part of the twentieth century.

He was born John Eckert about fifty miles west of Toronto, Ontario, Canada, in 1869. His parents had emigrated individually from Bavaria, met and married in Ontario. John was the middle of their nine children. It was a devout Catholic family. Attendance at Mass meant a six-mile horseback ride. If weather prevented that, they and their neighbors would gather for Sunday services.

As John grew up, he was attracted to the Capuchin community after two Capuchin friars preached a mission at the family's parish church. First he joined the Third Order Franciscans at St. Jerome's Seminary. Then he spent some time with the Franciscan community at St. Bonaventure Monastery in Detroit, finally deciding to enter the novitiate there in 1891. He was given the religious name Stephen. After a year there, he studied for four years at the major seminary at St. Francis Friary in Milwaukee. While there he trained himself to be a good preacher, listening to sermons and then discussing them with his fellow seminarians.

He was ordained a priest on July 2, 1896. For the next seventeen years, he was given numerous short assignments in New York City and Yonkers in the East, Detroit and Fond-du-Lac in the Midwest, and back to several parishes in New York. During most of that time, he conducted retreats or served as a hospital chaplain. During all his assignments he was credited with bringing many fallen-away Catholics back to the Church through home visitations, distributing Catholic literature in public places, and preaching retreats, especially for men. He also reached out to non-Catholics and made hundreds of converts.

His first experience with African-Americans came when he was serving in St. John the Baptist Church in midtown Manhattan in 1896. In 1897, while in Yonkers, he traveled to Philadelphia to learn more about them from the Sisters of the Blessed Sacrament, the community that Mother Katharine Drexel (now Saint Katharine) had founded in 1891 to work among Indians and African-Americans.

In 1905, Father Stephen expressed to his superiors an interest in starting an itinerant ministry among blacks in the South. His superiors investigated the possibility, but it was rejected by the superior general in Rome. In 1907, back at St. John's Church in New York, he worked among the black population in addition to his other duties.

In 1911, Archbishop Sebastian Messmer of Milwaukee established St. Benedict the Moor Mission for the Colored and entrusted it to the Capuchin Friars. This was the apostolate Father Eckert was looking for. In 1913 he was assigned to that mission.

In his book *Saints of North America*, Father Vincent O'Malley wrote,

> Father Stephen continued in this mission what he had done in previous missions, but this time for the African-Americans for whom he felt a great affection and calling. He visited hundreds of families. The school enrollment grew by leaps and bounds. To attract students from a wider geographical base Father Stephen conceived of, constructed, and fund-raised for a

boarding school. To ensure a future for all the graduates, the priest-founder instituted both academic and vocational tracks. Ahead of his time, he opened a day nursery for working mothers, and a residence and employment agency for young women. He begged locally and preached nationally to promote and provide for the school.

He also experienced criticism among some of the laity for his affection for the black community and from some of his brother priests for what they considered financial folly in trying to fund a boarding school, a nursery school, and a residence for women. But he continued, seemingly untiringly.

After ten years at St. Benedict the Moor, he contracted pneumonia and died on February 16, 1923, at age fifty-three.

A life-size statue of Father Eckert was erected at St. Benedict the Moor Mission's churchyard. The inscription reads, "Apostle and Champion of the Colored Race."

CHAPTER TWENTY-THREE

NELSON BAKER

Father Nelson Baker accomplished an amazing amount of good, thanks to Our Lady of Victory—and natural gas.

He developed his devotion to Our Lady of Victory when, as a seminarian, he made a pilgrimage to Notre Dame des Victoires in Paris. He promised Mary that he would promote devotion to her under that title. But we're getting ahead of our story because he was already thirty-two when that happened.

Nelson was born in 1842 to an Irish-Catholic mother and a German-Catholic father, a grocer in Buffalo, New York. Biographers describe him as a mischievous boy as he was growing up. One night he and a younger brother went to the offices of the local Republican Party, which was located on the second floor of the Baker home, and lowered the Republican flag. They then ran to the Democratic Party offices, lowered its flag and replaced it with the Republican one, and then returned to put the Democratic flag on the Republican flagpole. The next day they watched gleefully at the commotion they caused when the switch was discovered.

The family worshiped at St. Patrick's Church and Nelson joined the St. Vincent de Paul Society.

During the Civil War, Nelson joined the Army and was sent to Gettysburg and then to New York City, where he helped deal with the draft riots. After the war, he returned to Buffalo where he and another man began a grain and feed business. When he was twenty-six, though, he started to feel the call to the priesthood and began Latin classes. After taking a Great Lakes steamer cruise in the summer of 1869, he enrolled in the Seminary and College of Our Lady of the Angels. He made that pilgrimage to Notre Dame des Victoires in Paris in 1874, two years before his ordination.

After his ordination he was assigned to St. Patrick's Parish on Limestone Hill in West Seneca, now Lackawanna, New York. It included an orphanage and boys' home—both deeply in debt. Feeling frustrated as the young assistant pastor, he asked his bishop for a transfer, which was granted. A year later, though, the bishop, Stephen Ryan, asked him to return to St. Patrick's as pastor and to restore it to financial health.

He began a fund-raising campaign by developing a mailing list and writing for donations for the orphanage and boys' home. For those who responded, he founded the Association of Our Lady of Victory that donors could join at a cost of only twenty-five cents a year. To keep donors informed he began a newsletter that he called *The Appeal for Homeless and Destitute Children*. The campaign was outstandingly successful because, within two years, he was able to pay off the entire debt.

Donations continued and Father Baker used the money to expand the orphanage and build a trade school where the boys could learn a trade. In place of the newsletter he published a magazine, *The Annals of Our Lady of Victory*. He ordered a statue of Our Lady of Victory, which he placed in the orphanage's chapel.

Then, after hearing that natural gas had been discovered across the Niagara River in Canada, he wondered if perhaps there was natural gas on the church's property. Somehow he was able to convince his bishop to let him drill for it. When the drilling crew arrived, he buried a small statue of Our Lady of Victory about a foot into the ground and told them to dig as close to the statue as possible without touching it.

Drilling went on for months. Novenas were said, but no gas. Drilling continued—six hundred feet, eight hundred, one thousand. Then, on August 21, 1891, a stream of gas shot up from one thousand one hundred thirty-seven feet, lit an open forge and rocketed an eighty-foot flame into the sky.

Father Baker had the money he needed. He added a gym and recreation hall to his boys' home, and started a Working Boys Home where his vocational school graduates could live. In 1908 he was shocked to discover the bodies of two hundred abandoned babies in a sewer, so he constructed a home for abandoned infants (with a bassinet in the foyer where anyone could leave a baby). In 1915 he built a hospital for unwed mothers that he later turned into a general hospital.

In all, he built two dozen major buildings and at one point was housing and educating almost four hundred young boys and one hundred working boys. To feed them, he bought a two hundred seventy-five-acre farm. In all this work, he had the help of the Sisters of St. Joseph.

In 1921, when he was seventy-nine, he started building a shrine to Our Lady of Victory. Five years later, when Father Baker was celebrating his golden anniversary as a priest, Cardinal Patrick Hayes of New York dedicated the completely-paid-for Basilica of Our Lady of Victory.

Father Baker died in 1936 at age ninety-four. It was estimated that a half-million people attended his wake, at times walking four abreast for over a mile. Even at two o'clock in the morning it took a half hour to reach his bier. An archbishop, four bishops, and seven hundred priests were present for his funeral. *The Buffalo Times* summed up his accomplishments:

> To the hungry during his ministry he fed fifty million meals. During the Depression at one time he was serving more than a million meals a year. He gave away a million loaves of bread. He clothed the naked to the number of a half million. He gave medical care to two hundred fifty thousand and supplied medicines to two hundred thousand more. Three hundred thousand men, women and children received some sort of education or training at his hands. A hundred thousand boys were trained for trades. Six hundred

thousand unmarried mothers in their distress knocked at his door and did not knock in vain. More than six thousand destitute and abandoned babies were placed in foster homes.

All because of his devotion to Our Lady of Victory.

CHAPTER TWENTY-FOUR

ROSE HAWTHORNE LATHROP

Rose Hawthorne Lathrop was born in 1851, the daughter of novelist Nathaniel Hawthorne and Sophie Peabody, who traced her ancestry to the Mayflower at Plymouth Rock. Rose married George Parson Lathrop, editor of the *Atlantic Monthly*, and they had a son. She also became an acclaimed poet and short-story writer.

When she was twenty-nine, their four-year-old son died. When she was forty, she and George both converted to Catholicism. However, George became an alcoholic and, when Rose was forty-four, she separated from him. He died of liver disease three years later.

Through all this, Rose was searching for a greater purpose in life. Her parents had instilled in her a compassion for the poor and she greatly admired Saint Vincent de Paul and Father Damien de Veuster, the "leper priest" of Molokai. She finally found her calling when she realized the plight of cancer victims.

Cancer was thought to be a contagious disease in the late nineteenth century. Those with the disease were not treated in regular hospitals for fear of exposing other patients. Wealthy victims could hire nurses to come to their homes, but the poor couldn't do that. Things came to a head for Rose when she encountered a young girl with cancer who could not afford medical care and had to check herself in to New York's almshouse on Blackwell's Island in the middle of the East River. Besides cancer patients, there were convicted criminals, the insane, and others who were considered incurably ill.

After taking a three-month nursing course at New York Cancer Hospital, Rose moved to a small three-room tenement flat in New York's Lower East Side. From there she visited the cancerous poor, wrapped their bandages, cooked their meals and cleaned their homes. Soon she welcomed a few of the cancer victims into her home.

She realized that she needed help so she advertised in a newspaper, ending her appeal with, "Let the poor, the patient, the destitute, and the hopeless receive from our compassion what we would give to our own families." A woman named Alice Huber, thirty-six, saw the ad, contacted Rose and offered to help her one day a week. After three months, she moved into Rose's home. A month later, George Lathrop died.

In February 1899, a Dominican priest visiting the home noticed a statue of Saint Rose of Lima, Rose's patron saint. He suggested that the women consider becoming Dominican tertiaries, as Saint Rose was. With the approval of Archbishop John Corrigan, they did, with Rose taking the religious name Mother Alphonsa and Alice, Sister Rose. A year later the archbishop permitted them to wear the Dominican habit, pronounce vows, and form a community they called the Servants of Relief for Incurable Cancer.

Meanwhile, a wealthy benefactor who learned about the sisters' work provided a new home for them, adequate for the women patients. The men patients, though, had to be put up in nearby tenements.

In 1901, the women learned about a large piece of property for sale, thirty miles north of New York in Sherman Park. It belonged to French Dominican nuns who had returned to France. With the help of wealthy friends, the women bought nine acres of land. It included a sixty-room building suitable for their patients that Mother Alphonsa named St. Rose's Home. Thanks to donated services of doctors, their work with cancer patients flourished. In 1902 the townspeople changed the name of their town from Sherman Park to Hawthorne in honor of Rose.

In 1912, the original building was razed and a new St. Rose's Home was built. Ten years later, though, a fire at Christmas time burned down the home. Mother Alphonsa raised almost a quarter of a million dollars to replace the home, most of it through a periodical she founded called *Christ's Poor*. She made it a rule never to charge any of her patients to ensure that money was never a factor when it came to patients' care. She sought and accepted donations from the general public and from wealthy benefactors, but not from patients, their relatives, or the government.

She continued her work for the cancerous poor until her death in 1926 at age seventy-five. By then her community had grown to thirty-one members.

CHAPTER TWENTY-FIVE

JAMES WALSH and THOMAS PRICE

Fathers James A. Walsh and Thomas F. Price were the co-founders of the Catholic Foreign Mission Society of America, commonly known as Maryknoll.

At the beginning of the twentieth century, the United States was considered mission territory, not a country that would send missionaries to other countries. Its jurisdiction still rested in the Sacred Congregation of Propaganda Fide in Rome, the congregation for the missions. Europeans were accustomed to coming to the United States, or sending money for the missions here.

Father Walsh, though, thought it was time to instill in Americans a greater awareness of the need for mission work. He had grown up in Boston, the son of immigrants who had been born in County Cork, Ireland, had come to the United States as children, met and married in Boston. He studied at both Boston College and Harvard

University before entering the seminary in 1886. After his ordination in 1892, he was assigned to St. Patrick's Parish in Roxbury. In 1903 he was appointed director of the Society for the Propagation of the Faith in Boston.

In 1904 he presented a paper in Washington to priests involved in missionary work in this country. He said that home missions would prosper if American Catholics would develop an international vision of mission. Father Price was in the audience, and he became intrigued with the idea. The two men spoke after the presentation. No more was done at that time, but the two priests began to exchange correspondence.

Father Price had been born in 1860 in North Carolina to non-Catholic parents; his father was Episcopalian and his mother Methodist. Both parents converted to Catholicism and two of Thomas's sisters became Sisters of Mercy and a brother also became a priest. The pastor of his parish, Father James Gibbons, encouraged Thomas to consider a vocation to the priesthood and Thomas enrolled at St. Charles Seminary in Ellicott City, Maryland, later transferring to St. Mary's Seminary in Baltimore.

While he was a seminarian, he was on a passenger ship that crashed in a storm. He believed that he was saved by the Blessed Virgin, who led him to a piece of floating debris until he could be rescued.

Thomas was ordained a priest in 1886, six years before Father Walsh. He then spent twenty-five years as an itinerant missionary in North Carolina, traveling by horse and buggy to visit the few Catholics in that state, and trying to convert the non-Catholics. For that purpose, in 1897 he founded the magazine *Truth*, which attained a circulation of seventeen thousand. He also founded an orphanage and the magazine *The Orphan Boy* to earn income for the orphanage.

In 1906, Father Walsh and a few other priests (but not Father Price) established the Catholic Foreign Mission Bureau to publish books about the missions. It also published the country's first missionary magazine, *The Field Afar*.

It happened, providentially, that both Father Walsh and Father Price attended the Eucharistic Congress in Montreal in 1910. They met again and, before the congress was over, started plans for the foundation of a foreign mission seminary. They knew, of course, that they would have to have the backing of the American hierarchy.

Fortunately, Father Price had connections. By this time, his former pastor, for whom he had served at Mass in North Carolina and who had encouraged him in his vocation, was Cardinal

James Gibbons, Archbishop of Baltimore. Another priest, who had been his classmate in the seminary, was now Archbishop William O'Connell of Boston. Father Price wrote to him, asking that he release Father Walsh from the archdiocese so he could help develop the foreign mission society. The request was granted.

Cardinal Gibbons enthusiastically supported the priests' plan. He wrote to all the U.S. archbishops asking for their approval, saying that American Catholics could not delay participation in foreign missions "lest our own faith should suffer." The archbishops unanimously approved the plan and sent the two priests to Rome. On June 29, 1911, the Congregation for the Propagation of the Faith approved the bishops' recommendation and the next day Pope Pius X blessed the new work.

The priests returned to the United States and purchased a property near Ossining, New York, overlooking the Hudson River. Father Walsh, named the society's first administrator, called it "Maryknoll" since it was on a hilltop.

The two founders didn't always agree with each other. Father Price wanted his North Carolina missions to be included in the scope of the new society, but Father Walsh and Cardinal Gibbons insisted on keeping the focus on foreign missions. Father Price also wanted the Philippines and Latin America to be included, but Father Walsh preferred to limit the scope of the new society to areas then under the auspices of the Propagation of the Faith. As administrator, Father Walsh's decisions prevailed. Father Price became the society's chief recruiter and fundraiser, traveling in the eastern part of the United States and in the Midwest.

In 1917, Father Walsh traveled to the Far East to select an area for the first mission. He chose an area in China. The next year three newly-ordained priests were ready to be sent to China. Father Walsh asked Father Price to lead them and serve as superior. He did and worked in Yeungkong, China for nine months until he suffered an infected appendix. He died in Hong Kong on September 12, 1919. He was buried there, but his remains were taken back to Maryknoll in 1936.

Father Price was known for his special devotion to the Blessed Virgin, especially after he believed that she had saved him after that shipwreck. He visited the shrine of Our Lady of Lourdes in France four times. Beginning in 1908 until the day of his death, he wrote daily letters to Mary, the letters totaling three thousand eighty-seven.

Father Walsh continued to lead the society. In 1933 Pope Pius XI named him titular bishop of

Siene. During his episcopal ordination in Rome, he felt fatigued, but continued his usual busy pace until his death at Maryknoll on April 14, 1936. By then, twenty-five years after its founding, Maryknoll had grown to more than two hundred fifty members with missions in China, Japan, Korea, the Philippines and Hawaii. With missions in the Philippines, Father Price had gotten his way.

The two founders are buried side by side at Maryknoll.

CHAPTER TWENTY-SIX

MARIE-CLEMENT STAUB

J oseph Staub grew up in Alsace with a great devotion to the Sacred Heart of Jesus and to Saint Joan of Arc, who had been from Lorraine, which bordered Alsace. Both were to figure prominently in his life.

Joseph joined the Assumptionist Fathers in 1896 and took the religious name Marie-Clement in honor of the Blessed Virgin and his father. After studies in Louvain and Rome, during which he earned doctorates in philosophy and theology, he was ordained a priest in 1904. After several initial assignments, including a year in England, he was sent to the United States in 1909. His primary assignment was as chaplain at an orphanage in Worcester, Massachusetts, but his superiors gave him permission to preach on devotion to the Sacred Heart.

Father Staub had developed a strong devotion to the Sacred Heart while a youth. A picture of the Sacred Heart had a prominent place in his family's home and the seminary he attended was dedicated to the Sacred Heart. Shortly before his birth, the bishops of France had dedicated that country to the Sacred Heart. It was natural that, as a young priest, he would write about devotion to the Sacred Heart and he preached about this devotion while he was superior of a high school seminary during that year in England.

One of his biographers, Serge Saint-Michel, wrote of him, "He spoke with such conviction, such enthusiasm and love. His one desire was to spread love like a blazing fire, that the whole world might be plunged into the burning, loving Heart of Jesus."

Mainly through his efforts, thousands joined the Archconfraternity of Prayer and Penance in honor of the Sacred Heart of Jesus. When Father Staub met with Pope Pius X in 1914, he presented him a list of twenty thousand members. By 1919, that number exceeded one hundred thousand. The Archconfraternity tried to enthrone the Sacred Heart in homes, schools and businesses, and was highly successful in that part of the twentieth century. Members prayed to the Sacred Heart and did penance.

But Father Staub also had great devotion to Saint Joan of Arc, especially after she was beatified in 1909. He attended her canonization in 1920 but even before that he was seeking donations to build an altar in her honor at Assumption College in Worcester. While he was doing that, in 1913, a rectory housekeeper in Fitchburg, Massachusetts, Alice Caron, told him that Saint Joan wanted more than that from him. "She wants you to provide a community of Sisters, who will offer themselves as victims of love to the Sacred Heart for the benefit of priests," she told him.

Father Staub met with Alice and two other women on Christmas Eve of 1914, and with them plus four other women on New Year's Eve. The result of those meetings was the founding of the Sisters of St. Joan of Arc in a cottage near Assumption College. Father Staub provided direction and vision to the community.

He continued his preaching in both the United States and Canada. In 1917 he expanded the sisters' community into Canada, near Quebec. In 1920 the community received its formal episcopal and papal approval. In 1928 he established foundations in France, where the sisters became known as the Lorraines, in reference to Joan of Arc's birthplace. They obtained the castle at Beaulieu-les-Fontaines where Joan of Arc had been imprisoned for nine days. They converted the dungeon into a shrine.

Father Staub continued to preach devotion to the Sacred Heart and to care for the community he founded until his death in 1936. At that time, the community had one hundred thirty-nine members serving in thirty-four houses in the United States, Canada and France.

CHAPTER TWENTY-SEVEN

MIRIAM TERESA DEMJANOVICH

Like Saint Thérèse of Lisieux, Miriam Teresa Demjanovich led a relatively hidden life in a convent and died young. Saint Thérèse was twenty-four when she died and Teresa was twenty-six.

Teresa was born in 1901 in Bayonne, New Jersey, to immigrants from Slovakia, the youngest of seven children. After graduating from high school at age sixteen, she spent two years caring for her sick mother. After her mother's death, she entered the College of St. Elizabeth in Morristown, New Jersey, operated by the Sisters of Charity. She excelled scholastically and was one of only two students from her class to graduate *summa cum laude.*

She taught English and Latin at the Academy of St. Aloysius in Jersey City, but after a year of that realized that teaching was not her vocation. She had long been interested in the life of a religious, so in 1924 she began to seek a religious community. First she visited the Carmelite community in the Bronx, but the Carmelites weren't willing to accept her because she had poor eyesight caused by oscillating pupils that gave her headaches. The Carmelites suggested that she wait a few more years.

She didn't wait. Late in 1924 she applied to the Sisters of Charity at Convent Station, New Jersey, and was accepted. She was supposed to enter the order on February 2, 1925, but her father caught a cold that developed into pneumonia and he died on January 30, so her entrance was postponed until February 11. After her postulancy, she became a novice and took the religious name Miriam.

Benedictine Father Benedict Bradley was the community's spiritual director and he quickly recognized Sister Miriam's spirituality as well as her writing ability. He encouraged her to write down her spiritual thoughts—much as Saint Therese's superior had encouraged her to do. Then Father Benedict, realizing that her spirituality was more profound than his own, asked if she would write conferences that Father Benedict would deliver as his own. With her superior's approval, she began to do that, preparing a new conference for Father

Benedict each week. The superior gave her time each week to prepare the conference, but the other sisters didn't know about it.

In November of 1926, Sister Miriam became ill. After a tonsillectomy, she returned to the convent but could barely walk to her room. After a few days she asked if she could return to the infirmary but her superior, thinking it odd that someone so young could be so sick, told her, "Pull yourself together!"

Father Benedict visited her right after the superior. Sister Miriam related what she had said to her and added, "Father, for a long time there has been nothing to pull."

When Father Benedict realized how sick she was, he notified her brother, who called their nurse-sister. She went to the convent and immediately took Sister Miriam to the hospital where she was diagnosed with "physical and nervous exhaustion, with myocarditis and acute appendicitis." Doctors, though, didn't think she was strong enough for an operation and her condition worsened. Her brother and sister asked permission for her to profess her vows and permission was granted. She died on May 8, 1927.

After her death, Father Benedict told the community that the conferences he had been giving had been written by Sister Miriam. The community immediately recognized her spiritual maturity, published the conferences in a book called *Greater Perfection*, and began her cause for canonization.

CHAPTER TWENTY-EIGHT

MARIA LUISA JOSEFA

Venerable Maria Luisa Josefa was Mexican rather than American, but I decided to include her in this book because she spent five years in Los Angeles. She and her Carmelite community fled there when Mexican President Plutarco Elias Calles enforced anti-Catholic laws in 1924. Church properties were confiscated and priests and nuns exiled. Many Mexicans were martyred and twenty-five of them, canonized in 2000, are included in my book *American Saints*.

Maria's parents owned an extensive ranch near Atotonilco el Alto, fifty miles east of Guadalajara, Mexico, where she was born in 1866. They called her Luisita. It was still the custom then for parents to choose a husband for their daughters and, when she was fifteen, they chose a physician, Pascual Rojas, who was thirty. They opened the first hospital at Atotonilco, which flourished under Luisa's leadership.

After fourteen years of marriage, during which they had been unable to have children, Pascual died. After his death, Luisa decided to fulfill a desire she long had had and entered the convent of the Discalced Carmelites of St. Teresa at Guadalajara, taking the religious name Maria.

Without her leadership, the hospital floundered and the townspeople asked Archbishop Jose de Jesus Ortiz Rodriguez to urge her to return. He did and, after much prayer, she believed that it was God's will for her to return to the hospital. She also opened a school for poor girls and volunteers soon joined her in this work.

In 1904, Maria and seven of the volunteers dedicated themselves to caring for the poor. Three years later, there were twenty women. A new archbishop, Francisco Orozco y Jimenez, then told them that, if they were living like religious, they should become religious and he recommended the Sisters Servants of the Blessed Sacrament. So Maria again left the hospital, taking nineteen women with her.

Without these women, the inevitable happened—the hospital was again nearly collapsing. Within months, the archbishop told Maria that she must return to her work of caring for the sick and educating the young. So once again she obeyed the archbishop, but only five of the nineteen women returned with her.

Just as before, when Maria restored the hospital and school, young women joined her. And, just as before, the archbishop accused the women of trying to live as nuns. This time he suggested that Maria should found a third-order Carmelite community, with the sisters wearing the Carmelite habit but spending time doing apostolic work. In 1920, the Vatican approved this community and Maria Luisa founded the Carmelite Sisters of the Sacred Heart.

Four years later she and her sisters fled to Los Angeles, where Maria began another foundation of her community. She returned to Mexico in 1929, after President Calles was overthrown and sought refuge in the United States. She worked there until her death in 1937.

Father Vincent O'Malley wrote in *Saints of North America*: "Her life evidences development in personality and flexibility in responding to the changing demands of times, archbishops, and governments. Wife, widow, in and out of two religious communities, and foundress of a Carmelite community with two branches, she leaves a legacy of trying to discover and do God's will."

CHAPTER TWENTY-NINE

MARIA KAUPAS

Catholics in Lithuania had to practice their religion underground when Casimira Kaupas, born in 1880, was growing up. Russia ruled two-thirds of Lithuania and had ever since Empress Catherine II seized the territory in 1795. The czars decreed the Russian Orthodox Church the state religion and closed Catholic churches, monasteries and parishes. The Lithuanian people revolted in 1863, unsuccessfully, and persecution against them was intensified. Both priests and laity participated in the underground movement. Casimira's father, at risk of imprisonment, helped smuggle Catholic literature from Prussia into Lithuania.

Meanwhile, Lithuanians who had managed to immigrate to the United States were writing to their relatives still in Lithuania, telling them about the freedom they were enjoying and urging them to come to America. In 1892, Casimira's brother, Anthony, left Lithuania and made his way to the United States, planning to become a priest and serve the Lithuanians in America. After his ordination in 1896, he was assigned to St. Joseph Lithuanian Church in Scranton, Pennsylvania. He wrote home to his parents to see if Casimira, seventeen at the time, would be willing to serve as his housekeeper. She was willing, and she traveled to Scranton in 1897.

After four years, though, she got homesick and returned to Lithuania. Four years later, now twenty-five, she was ready to return to the United States, but this time she wanted to become a teaching religious to help Lithuanian Americans practice their faith. First, though, she needed religious formation. A friend of her brother provided financial support and she went to Ingenbohl, Switzerland where she spent time with the Sisters of Mercy of the Holy Cross.

Believing herself ready, she asked her brother to identify a spiritual adviser for her intended community. He chose Father Anthony Staniukynas, who then asked Bishop John W. Shanahan of Harrisburg to sponsor the new congregation. The bishop agreed and Casimira returned to the United States with two companions. Bishop Shanahan asked the Sisters of the Immaculate Heart of Mary in Scranton to provide further spiritual formation for the women. When he thought they were ready, the bishop approved the new religious community. The congregation of the Sisters of St. Casimir was founded on August 29, 1907. Bishop Shanahan gave Casimira the religious name Maria.

When Sister Maria took her perpetual vows in 1913, she was elected superior general and was thereafter called Mother Maria. She led the community for twenty-seven years, until her death. By that time the community had grown to more than three hundred forty sisters living in more than thirty houses.

The congregation's first school was in Mount Carmel, Pennsylvania, sixty miles from Scranton. However, as the community grew, it moved its motherhouse to Chicago, which had the largest concentration of Lithuanian immigrants. The sisters began schools in Chicago and Waukegan, Illinois, and in Philadelphia and Newtown, Pennsylvania.

In 1927, Cardinal George Mundelein asked the sisters to operate Holy Cross Hospital in Chicago when Lithuanian Catholic Charities could no longer do so. In 1937 the community started schools in New Mexico. Mother Maria made plans to expand to Argentina, but that happened a year after her death.

After the Lithuanian people gained their

freedom from Russia at the end of World War I, Lithuania's bishops asked Mother Maria to expand the Sisters of St. Casimir to her homeland. She did, with four of her sisters opening a convent and school in Pazaislis. Fourteen years later, though, the Lithuanian branch separated from the American community because the bishop wanted it to be a diocesan community.

When she was fifty-three, Mother Maria contracted breast cancer, which advanced to bone cancer. She survived to age sixty and died in 1940.

CHAPTER THIRTY

EMIL KAPAUN

Father Emil Kapaun was an Army chaplain who died May 23, 1951 at age thirty-five in a Chinese POW camp during the Korean War. He is buried somewhere along the Yalu River in North Korea. As he was being carried away to die, while suffering intense pain, he told his fellow prisoners, "If I don't come back, tell my bishop that I died a happy death."

He was born in 1916 in Pilsen, Kansas. He was ordained a priest in 1940 and, during World War II, served as an Army chaplain in China and Burma. In 1949 he was sent to Japan and in 1950 to Korea.

He was captured by the Chinese on November 2, 1950 as he was giving the last rites to a dying soldier. During the next six months and twenty-one days he did everything he could to minister to his fellow prisoners' spiritual and physical needs.

The prisoners suffered from wretched and unsanitary conditions, with a meager and unhealthy diet. Father Kapaun soon learned that they had to steal food or slowly starve to death. He risked his life by sneaking into fields around the prison to look for hidden potatoes and sacks of corn. While other prisoners kept guards occupied, he would sneak into a supply shed, grab a sack of cracked corn and scurry off into the bushes.

But the men continued to die. The POWs had to bury their own dead and Father Kapaun always volunteered to do it, praying for their souls as he dug their graves. He buried them naked, taking their clothing to help warm the living. He washed the foul undergarments of the dead and distributed them to men who could barely move because of dysentery.

Enlisted men POWs were held in their own huts and Father Kapaun learned how to escape to visit them. He would lead a quick prayer service before giving a short sermon, urging the men not to lose hope and not to fall for the doctrines the Chinese were trying to indoctrinate them with. A prisoner who survived, First Lieutenant Mike Dowe, said that Father Kapaun's presence turned a stinking, louse-ridden hut—for a little while—into a cathedral.

The prisoners were forced to sit for hours to

listen to lectures by "Comrade Sun," a fanatic who hated Americans. According to Lieutenant Dowe, "Father was not openly arrogant, nor did he use subterfuge. Without losing his temper or raising his voice, he'd answer the lecturer point by point, with a calm logic that set Comrade Sun screaming and leaping on the platform like an angry ape."

Father Kapaun was never punished, although he was threatened, and it soon became evident, Lieutenant Dowe said, that "the Chinese were afraid of him. They recognized in him a strength they could not break, a spirit they could not quell."

Eventually, though, Father Kapaun battled dysentery, pneumonia and a blood clot in one of his legs. The Chinese carried him away to what served as a hospital, where he died.

CHAPTER THIRTY-ONE

SOLANUS CASEY

No man born in the United States has yet
been canonized or beatified. However,
Capuchin Franciscan Father Solanus
Casey is the first male born in the United States
to be declared "Venerable," the step below beatification. Naturally, it is hoped that he will soon
be declared blessed.

Father Solanus died in 1957. Therefore,
numerous people living today met him and were
perhaps cured of an illness through his prayers. I
met him during my teen years while he was living
for ten years at St. Felix Friary in Huntington,
Indiana, where I grew up.

He was born in Prescott, Wisconsin, on November 25, 1870, the sixth of sixteen children of
Bernard and Ellen Casey, both Irish immigrants
when they were children. He was named after
his father and, like his father, was called Barney
as he grew up.

The Caseys practiced all the Catholic devotions that were common at the time, including regular family prayers. As an adult, the rosary was seldom far from his hand and he prayed it often each day.

In 1878 black diphtheria struck the neighborhood and the Casey family. Two of the children died and Barney had a severe case that made his voice weak, wispy, and high-pitched for the rest of his life.

Barney tried to become a diocesan priest but his grades were so poor that he was asked to leave the seminary. Then he learned about the Capuchins and was accepted at their novitiate in Milwaukee. He was given the religious name Solanus in honor of a Spanish Franciscan who worked in South America in the seventeenth century. His grades there, though, were not much better—mainly because classes were taught in German and Latin. His superiors finally decided to ordain him, but as a "simplex priest," without faculties to hear confessions or preach formal sermons.

His first assignment was in Yonkers, New York. As a simplex priest, he was assigned to be porter, welcoming people when they arrived at the monastery. It wasn't long before word got out that Father Solanus had the gift of healing, a gift that he was quick to deny. "Only God can heal," he insisted. But the people were healed through Father Solanus's intercession. He also had the gift of prophecy, frequently telling about things that would happen in the future.

After fourteen years at Yonkers, he continued his ministry of porter in Manhattan for six years and then at St. Bonaventure Monastery in Detroit for twenty-one years. Thousands of people came to see him and he patiently met with all of them, often skipping his meals to do so. He ate sparingly anyway and seldom found time for sleep. He also became involved in various social justice causes, especially during the Depression, and promoted devotion to Mary by endorsing a three-volume work called *The Mystical City of God*.

He was transferred to St. Michael's in Brooklyn in 1945 and then to St. Felix Monastery in Huntington, Indiana, in 1946. That was his last assignment, when he was semi-retired but still answering forty to fifty letters a day. He returned to Detroit in 1956, where he died on July 31, 1957 at age eighty-six.

Father Solanus was noted not only for the hundreds of healings that took place through his prayers, but also for the extraordinary way he practiced the virtues, perhaps especially the virtue of humility.

Father Benedict Joseph Groeschel is widely

known for his devotional books and for his appearances on the Eternal Word Television Network. Although he is the founder of the Franciscan Friars of the Renewal, he began as a Capuchin. When he was a novice, he came to know Father Solanus. He has written about coming across Father Solanus deeply in prayer in the chapel at 3 o'clock in the morning, completely oblivious to his presence.

Father Benedict also wrote that, in the course of his life, he had had the opportunity to know and observe several people known for their holiness. Nevertheless, he said, "Father Solanus was the most extraordinary. I could easily say without any hesitation that he was the greatest human being I have ever known."

That is why this very simple priest could become the first native-born American to be beatified or canonized.

CHAPTER THIRTY-TWO

MARY VIRGINIA MERRICK

Mary Virginia Merrick served the Christ Child despite spending most of her life confined to bed or a wheelchair.

She was born on November 2, 1866 to a prominent Washington, D.C. family, descendants of the Calvert family of Maryland. Her parents raised her as a devout Catholic. She often accompanied her mother on visits, with gifts, to the homes of the disadvantaged.

During her teen years, Mary Virginia fell from the window of a playhouse. The accident sentenced her to a life in a reclining position with painful and restricted movement. That didn't stop her from serving others.

In 1884, she learned that an impoverished family was expecting a baby at Christmas time. She invited her sisters and friends to join her in sewing a layette for the baby. The baby girl, named Mary, became the recipient of Mary Virginia's first organized act of love. She continued to sew clothes for needy children and encouraged others to join her.

There was also a little boy named Paul, the son of the Merrick family laundress. He liked to run errands for Mary Virginia. When she asked him what he wanted for Christmas, he replied that he wanted a red wagon, but he knew he couldn't get one because his father was out of work and there wouldn't be any Christmas presents.

Mary Virginia suggested that Paul write a letter to the Christ Child and ask for the red wagon.

The boy said, "Who's he?"

She replied, "He is the giver of all good gifts."

So Paul, though puzzled, wrote his letter. A couple of days later he returned not only with his letter but also with a handful of letters written by his brothers, sisters and playmates.

Naturally, Mary Virginia and her sisters and friends fulfilled the children's wishes. When they gave them to the children, the presents all had tags on them that read, "From the Christ Child."

These first gifts to children so delighted Mary Virginia that in 1887 she founded the Christ Child Society to assist impoverished children. By 1898 the society claimed more than three hundred members. The society was officially incorporated in 1903, by which time Christ Child Centers were open throughout Washington.

In the early twentieth century, branches of the society were operating as far away as Omaha, New York City and Chicago. In 1916, they were federated into a national organization. Today there are forty chapters and more than seven thousand one hundred members in eighteen states and the District of Columbia.

Mary Virginia Merrick died on January 10, 1955, when she was eighty-nine. At that time the Christ Child Society had stretched all the way across the country, from New York to California. They were all founded by a woman who suffered through her paralysis with a determination to serve God by serving poor children.

Throughout her life, when she was faced with scarce financial resources for the society, she replied simply, "The Christ Child will provide."

CHAPTER THIRTY-THREE

DOROTHY DAY

Although Dorothy Day always had a passion for social justice, the first part of her life was not what you would expect of a potential saint.

When she was born in 1897, the third of five children, her parents were infrequent worshipers at an Episcopalian church. As a child, she did believe in God and said night prayers by her bed. The family moved from Brooklyn to San Francisco, and later to Chicago. She had a brilliant intellect, enough to win a full scholarship to the University of Illinois at Urbana in 1914. While there, she joined the Socialist Party.

After two years in college, though, she dropped out and moved back to New York. She began to write for socialist periodicals called *The Call, The Masses,* and *The Liberator*, eventually becoming a free-lance writer.

She lived a bohemian lifestyle in Greenwich

Village with others who advocated radical social change in opposition to all organized government. Many of her friends joined the Communist Party, but she did not because it advocated violence in labor confrontations and adhered to an atheistic and anti-religious line. She became involved in the women's suffrage movement and ended up in jail for the first time after protesting in front of the White House in 1917. She spent thirty days in jail, ten of which she spent on a hunger strike. This was the first of many arrests and five imprisonments.

When the United States entered the First World War, Dorothy studied nursing and worked for a time at Kings County Hospital in Brooklyn. She soon realized, though, that her true vocation was writing, rather than nursing.

Her bohemian lifestyle included many romantic affairs, one of which ended with an abortion. She briefly married Barkeley Tobey, with whom she traveled for a year to London, Paris and throughout Italy, writing as she traveled. After her marriage broke up, she moved briefly to Chicago, working as a sales clerk, waitress and model for art classes, all the time continuing to write.

In 1923 her first book, an autobiographical novel she titled *The Eleventh Virgin*, was published. When a movie company bought movie rights to the book for five thousand dollars, she used the money to purchase a beach home in Staten Island. She invited a man named Forster Battleham to move in with her. They became the parents of a girl they named Tamar when Dorothy was twenty-eight.

The birth of her child changed her life. She later wrote in *The Long Loneliness: An Autobiography*, "I was not going to have her floundering through many years as I had done, doubting and hesitating, undisciplined and amoral." She was determined to have the baby baptized a Catholic because Dorothy had become attracted to the Catholic Church for its liturgy and devotions, and because it was "the Church of the immigrants, the Church of the poor." She thought that having her child baptized "was the greatest thing I could do for my child." Tamar was baptized in July of 1927.

Dorothy had, in fact, long been impressed with the Catholic Church. While she lived in Brooklyn she had attended Sunday Mass with a nurse friend, and in Chicago her three roommates also attended Mass. While she was living in New Orleans for a time, she regularly attended Sunday night Benediction at St. Louis Cathedral in Jackson Square. She began to pray the rosary, a devotion she was to continue the rest of her life.

However, Forster Battleham, with whom she was living, was an atheist who refused to talk about marriage. Dorothy realized that, if she were to practice the Catholic religion, she could no longer continue to live with him out of wedlock. She wrote, "I loved him. It was killing me to think of leaving him." But she did, on December 27, 1927. The next day she was received into the Catholic Church. She reformed her personal life while remaining just as passionate about social justice.

On December 8, 1932, she covered a labor protest in Washington as a journalist. While doing so, she kept wondering where the Catholic leadership was in the fight for justice for the workers. While in Washington, she went from the White House to the National Shrine of the Immaculate Conception. She prayed "that some way would open up for me" to work more effectively for the poor. When she returned to New York and entered her apartment, a man who introduced himself as Peter Maurin was sitting there. He had read Dorothy's articles and was convinced that they should work together. It was the answer to Dorothy's prayer.

They co-founded the Catholic Worker Movement in early 1933. Their first project was a newspaper. Peter proposed the name *The Catholic Radical* but Dorothy didn't like that title.

The Catholic Worker first appeared on May 1, 1933—May Day. Its purpose, as Dorothy wrote in the first issue, was "to popularize and make known the encyclicals of the popes in regard to social justice and the program put forth by the Church for the 'reconstruction of the social order.'" They began to sell the newspaper for a penny apiece at Union Square. They printed twenty-five hundred copies of the first issue, but by the end of 1933 the circulation grew to one hundred thousand. Within three years, the newspaper reached a circulation of one hundred eighty thousand.

The next project was to provide hospitality to the needy. Dorothy and Peter founded Hospitality Houses for the poor. By 1936, thirty-three Hospitality Houses were operating from coast to coast. Those who were taken in became part of the family. As she was to tell Margaret Gabriel, as quoted in an article in *St. Anthony Messenger* (April, 2003), "We let them stay forever. They live with us, they die with us, and we give them a Christian burial. We pray for them after they are dead.… They are our brothers and sisters in Christ."

Then, beginning in 1935, Catholic Worker Farms were started in five places: Easton, Pennsylvania; Newburg, New York; Staten Island, New York; and in the Hudson Valley villages of Tivoli and Marlboro.

Dorothy was an ardent pacifist, calling war a "tearing asunder of the body of Christ." When she refused to back General Francisco Franco during the Spanish Civil War as most of the U.S. hierarchy did, especially Cardinal Francis Spellman of New York, circulation of *The Catholic Worker* suffered. Parishes and schools that had been purchasing subscriptions canceled and circulation plunged from about two hundred thousand to fifty thousand.

In 1963 Dorothy went to Rome with a group of fifty Mothers for Peace to thank Pope John XXIII for his encyclical *Pacem in Terris*. She returned to Rome while the Second Vatican Council was in progress to plead with the pope and the bishops to condemn all wars. The council didn't do that, but its *Constitution on the Church in the Modern World (Gaudium et Spes)* did condemn nuclear war and military actions against non-combatants.

She continued to write for *The Catholic Worker*, a total of more than a thousand articles, plus about three hundred fifty articles for other magazines. She authored seven books, including *From Union Square to Rome*, about her spiritual journey to the Catholic Church, and her autobiography, *The Long Loneliness*. A list of the causes she supported includes garment industry employees, streetcar operators, iron workers, farm workers, seamen, prisoners, and conscientious objectors to military conscription. She supported Cesar Chavez and his farm workers and was jailed for the last time in 1973 after joining in a picket for his union.

She was frequently at odds with her archbishop, Cardinal Spellman. As noted, he praised and supported Francisco Franco in Spain. As head of the Military Ordinariate, Cardinal Spellman supported the Vietnam War, which Dorothy opposed. Dorothy supported Catholic cemetery workers in a dispute with the Archdiocese of New York.

In 1976, when she was seventy-nine, she suffered a heart attack after returning to the Catholic Worker Farm in Tivoli from the Eucharistic Congress in Philadelphia, where she had spoken. (Mother Teresa and the future Pope John Paul II were other speakers at the congress.) After her heart attack, Dorothy slowed down and didn't write or speak much during the last four years of her life. She died in 1980 at age eighty-three.

CHAPTER THIRTY-FOUR

ANGELINE McCRORY

Brigid McCrory was born in 1893 to a Catholic family in Ulster, Northern Ireland and grew up amid the hardships of that Protestant-dominated country. The family emigrated from there to Scotland when she was eight. When she was nineteen she entered the Little Sisters of the Poor, whose mission then, as now, was to care for the indigent elderly. She later explained her motivation in entering that order as her association with her elderly grandfather. "As a child, I remember that I always thought of the elderly as lonely, hungry, and cold, and my heart went out in sympathy to them," she said.

She received the religious name Sister Angeline Teresa of Saint Agathe. After professing her vows, Sister Angeline was assigned to a home in Brooklyn, arriving in the United States in 1915. After nine years of caring for the sick and begging for food for the sisters and their patients, she was named superior of Our Lady's Home in the Bronx. Now known as Mother Angeline, she was responsible for eighteen sisters and two hundred thirty elderly residents.

The rule for the Little Sisters was that their homes must accept only the indigent poor, but Mother Angeline interpreted "poor" broadly, welcoming elderly people who had some money but no companionship or joy. All went well for several years, until the Little Sisters of the Poor's mother general visited from France in 1927. She ordered Mother Angeline to adhere strictly to the rule.

Mother Angeline prayed about the situation and held discussions with others, trying to discern what she should do. She was convinced that the rules that might work well in France had to be adapted to the situation in the United States. Two years later, and after two official canonical visitations, she decided that she was called to leave the Little Sisters and found a new community. Along with six other sisters, she departed from the community. There was no animosity, at least on Mother Angeline's part. She wrote that she had always loved her former congregation and valued the spiritual formation that she received as well as respect for the aging that she learned from the Little Sisters.

New York's Cardinal Patrick Hayes gave

the seven sisters the old rectory of St. Elizabeth's Parish in New York City and they moved there on September 3, 1929. They considered that date as the community's foundation day.

Two years later, Mother Angeline asked Father Lawrence Flanagan, provincial of the Carmelite Province of New York, if the sisters could affiliate with the Carmelite Order. He approved, as did Cardinal Hayes, and on July 16, 1931 the Church recognized the foundation of the Carmelite Sisters for the Aged and Infirm. The new order's constitution received papal approval in 1957.

The Carmelites moved into St. Patrick's Home in the Bronx in 1931. As both the number of sisters and the elderly continued to grow, the sisters expanded St. Patrick's Home seven times during the next four decades. In 1947, they moved their motherhouse to Avila-on-the-Hudson in Germantown, New York, one hundred miles north of New York City.

Mother Angeline served as superior general of the Carmelite Sisters for the Aged and Infirm for almost half a century, from 1929 to 1978. During that time the order grew to more than three hundred sisters serving in fifty sites in thirty dioceses in the United States, plus one each in Ireland and Scotland.

Mother Angeline wrote:

> We all know that labor done for God is high and holy, but it must not replace habitually the spiritual exercises of the Rule. We must, as Carmelites, lead a contemplative and active life, giving the required time to prayer which is more important than our work.

She died on her ninety-first birthday in 1984, after fourteen years as a Little Sister of the Poor and fifty-five years as a Carmelite.

CHAPTER THIRTY-FIVE

CATHERINE de HUECK DOHERTY

C atherine de Hueck was called "Baroness" because she was one for a while, but most of her life was lived among the poor.

She was born Catherine Kolyschkine to aristocrats in Russia in 1896. Her father was Russian Orthodox and her mother Lutheran. She traveled extensively as a child, because of her father's occupation, and received part of her education in Alexandria, Egypt and Istanbul, Turkey. She learned to speak six languages and understood three more. Her parents also taught her a love of God and the poor, regularly taking her with them when they visited the poor. While in Alexandria she studied in a school run by Catholic nuns and thus learned about Catholicism.

She married her cousin Baron Boris de Hueck in 1911, when she was only fifteen. World War I began three years later. It was followed by the Bolshevik Revolution in 1917. Boris and Catherine escaped to Finland with their lives, but little else. They endured poverty and near starvation before making their way to England in 1920. There she was received into the Catholic Church.

Catherine and Boris immigrated to Canada in 1921. Catherine gave birth to a son and supported the three of them by working as a laundress, waitress and lecturer. Boris, meanwhile, lived a dissolute life and had numerous extra-marital affairs. The couple separated in 1930 and eventually divorced.

Catherine moved into the slums of Toronto to serve the poor. She founded what she called Friendship House there. However, when rumors spread that she was a communist she left Toronto in 1938 and moved to Harlem in New York City. She opened a Friendship House there and became an advocate for civil rights and social justice. She opened other Friendship Houses in various U.S. cities.

During the Spanish Civil War and the first part of World War II, she went to Europe to work as a journalist for Catholic periodicals. She then returned to Friendship House in Harlem.

In 1940, Eddie Doherty heard about Friendship House and decided to write about it. He went to Harlem to see what Catherine was doing, and to interview her. At the time, he was America's best-known and highest-paid journalist (and one of my heroes when I was a young boy growing up with an interest in journalism, especially after I read his autobiography, *Gall and Honey*). He not only wrote about Catherine (including, much later, her biography, *Tumbleweed*), he fell in love with her.

They married in 1943 after Catherine's first marriage was annulled. Eddie had been married twice before, but his first wife died in the 1918 flu epidemic and his second wife died in a freak accident.

Unfortunately, Catherine had problems with some of Friendship House's staff, partly over her marriage to Eddie. When these could not be resolved, Catherine and Eddie moved to Combermere, Ontario, Canada in 1947. They founded a new rural apostolate there that they named Madonna House. It is a community of both laity and priests committed to living Gospel values. The members take vows of chastity, poverty and obedience but, except for the priests, remain lay men and women. Both Eddie and Catherine wrote articles and books to publicize Madonna House.

Eddie eventually went to the Holy Land where he studied for the priesthood in the Melkite Greek Catholic Church. Once ordained, he returned to Madonna House, where he died May 4, 1975.

Catherine wrote hundreds of articles and more than thirty books. By the time of her death in 1985 at age eighty-nine, there were two hundred members of the community living in twenty-two missionary field-houses on three continents.

CHAPTER THIRTY-SIX

FULTON J. SHEEN

Nobody in the Catholic Church before or since has had the success on television that Bishop Fulton J. Sheen had from February 1952 to April 1957. Still today people say that they wish we had another Bishop Sheen who could explain Catholic doctrine on TV as he did. But he was unique.

He won an Emmy in 1952 as "Most Outstanding Television Personality," quipping as he accepted his award, "I wish to thank my four writers, Matthew, Mark, Luke and John." He made the covers of *Time, TV Guide* and *Look* magazines. The *Time* story said that he was "perhaps the most famous preacher in the U.S., certainly America's best-known Roman Catholic priest, and the newest star of U.S. television."

He had five-and-a-half million viewers a week when he was on opposite Milton Berle ("Mr. Television") on NBC and Frank Sinatra on CBS.

Sinatra's program was canceled and Berle's went down ten rating points. Bishop Sheen's office was receiving twenty-five thousand letters a day, many of them with money for the missions.

Bishop Sheen's program was called *Life Is Worth Living.* He always appeared in his full episcopal regalia. Although the programs were in black and white in those early days of television, he still made an impressive appearance. Few people realized that the bishop was only five feet seven inches tall and weighed no more than a hundred forty pounds. A theatrical and flamboyant showman, he knew how to mix serious matters with corny jokes, when to move upstage, when and how to modulate his voice, and the timing of a pause. Actors such as Loretta Young and comedians such as Jackie Gleason marveled at his sense of timing. An actor named Ramon Estevez was so impressed with him that, with the bishop's permission, he changed his name to Martin Sheen.

Bishop Sheen's only prop was a blackboard that he made good use of. When the two-sided blackboard was out of camera range a stagehand would turn it over. When the bishop moved back to a clean blackboard, he would smilingly inform his viewers that "my angel, Skippy" had cleaned the board for him. He ended his talks with a benediction and his most famous phrase, "God love you."

On those shows he taught Catholic doctrine, the philosophy and theology of Saint Thomas Aquinas, and the evils of communism—not exactly a recipe for exciting TV. Despite that, his charismatic personality made the show a success.

Before he created a sensation on television, Bishop Sheen was already well known as a great preacher in Catholic circles because he was a regular speaker on radio's *The Catholic Hour* from 1930 to 1952. Millions of copies of those talks were distributed by the National Council of Catholic Men. One talk alone, *Queen of Seven Swords*, delivered in 1934, went through eleven editions by 1948.

He was also renowned for his writing. Besides the printed radio talks, over a period of fifty-four years he wrote sixty-six books (sixteen of his more popular works have been kept in print by ST PAULS / Alba House and a number of other titles are available as well from other publishers to this date), seven booklets, and fourteen pamphlets. He wrote two weekly syndicated columns, one for the secular press that ran for thirty years and the other, called "God Loves You," for the Catholic press. He also edited two magazines. He and his works seemed to be everywhere.

During most of this time, he was known as *Monsignor* Fulton J. Sheen. He was made a papal chamberlain (Very Reverend Monsignor) in 1934 and a domestic prelate (Right Reverend Monsignor) in 1935. He didn't become a bishop until 1951 when he was named an auxiliary bishop to Cardinal Francis J. Spellman of New York. He was given the title of archbishop in 1969 and named Assistant at the Pontifical Throne in 1976.

His primary job, though, had nothing to do with TV. From 1950 to 1966 he was director of the Society for the Propagation of the Faith, which supports the Church's missions. During those sixteen years the Society raised nearly two hundred million dollars. He increased donations from three-and-a-half million dollars per year when he became director in 1950 to nearly sixteen million dollars in 1965. He himself contributed more than ten million dollars of his personal earnings.

One of Bishop Sheen's biographers, Thomas C. Reeves, called him "the leading American Catholic of the twentieth century." The Internet *Catholic Daily* took a poll to see who people thought were the most important Catholics of the twentieth century. Archbishop Sheen came in fourth behind Pope John Paul II, Mother Teresa, and Saint Padre Pio. Archbishop Sheen was the top American.

Before he became a radio and television star, Father Fulton J. Sheen honed his skills by teaching philosophy and theology at the Catholic University of America for twenty-four years. During most of that time he taught two courses a semester, two days a week. This allowed him time to write his books and to become a popular speaker. *Time* magazine reported in 1940 that he filled one hundred fifty speaking engagements while teaching at Catholic University.

The man who was to become Archbishop Fulton J. Sheen was born Peter John Fulton Sheen in El Paso, Illinois, on May 8, 1895, the eldest child of Newt and Delia Sheen. The family moved to Peoria when he was five. He dropped his name Peter when he was in the first grade and was thereafter known as Fulton, his mother's maiden name.

Fulton attended Spalding Institute, a small Catholic high school in Peoria. As valedictorian of his graduating class in 1913, he delivered a memorable speech, an indication of things to come. He attended St. Viator College, a small college in Bourbonnais, Illinois. He joined the debate team and by his sophomore year was the star of the team. He also had his own column in the campus magazine.

After graduation in 1917, Fulton headed for St. Paul's Seminary in St. Paul, Minnesota, where he was immersed in neo-Thomism, the philosophy and theology of St. Thomas Aquinas. He was ordained a priest on September 19, 1919. He then continued his education: first at the Catholic University of America; then the University of Louvain in Belgium, where he received his Ph.D. with greatest distinction. Then he moved to Rome where he studied at both the Angelicum and the Gregorian universities.

In 1925 Longmans-Green and Company published his first book, *God and Intelligence*, which had been his dissertation. G.K. Chesterton wrote the introduction. Neither man knew that someday this young priest would be known as "the American Chesterton."

Father Sheen was thirty years old now, with extraordinary academic credentials. But he was still a priest of the Diocese of Peoria and Bishop Edmund Dunne called him back to the diocese and assigned him as a curate in one of the poorest parishes in Peoria. His sermons packed the church, he visited every home in the parish, and he was successful at winning converts and bringing people back to the Church.

He was there only eight months though. Bishop Dunne was quite aware that Father Sheen was destined for bigger things and, two years earlier, he had promised Catholic University that the priest could join its faculty. In making the assignment to the poor parish, he said, he was testing Father Sheen's obedience. He passed the test.

While he was teaching at the Catholic University of America, Msgr. Sheen began to give sermons in St. Patrick's Cathedral in New York, commuting from Washington to New York. He soon packed the cathedral and his reputation began to grow.

Besides becoming known as a great preacher and teacher, Msgr. Sheen became renowned for the hundreds of people who converted to Catholicism as a result of his efforts. Among his most famous converts were Clare Boothe Luce, Henry Ford II, and the former communists Louis Budenz and Bella Dodd. In his sermons and radio talks, he announced that he would give personal instruction to all who requested it, and many did request it.

By 1945 Monsignor Sheen was conducting regular classes for those interested in joining the Church. When he traveled from Washington to

New York for his *Catholic Hour* radio programs, potential converts would gather at the Roosevelt Hotel, where he stayed. Women from his staff would greet them and play audiotapes that Monsignor Sheen had prepared. Then he would appear to answer questions and talk to each individual. He also conducted convert classes in his home in Washington.

In 1948 New York's Cardinal Francis J. Spellman invited Monsignor Sheen to join him on a trip. Cardinal Spellman thought of Monsignor Sheen as his protégé. On that trip, both Cardinal Spellman and Monsignor Sheen kept diaries. They described huge crowds everywhere they stopped—in Hawaii, the Fiji Islands, Australia, New Zealand, Java, Singapore, the Philippines, China, and Japan. By the end of the trip, which lasted fifty-two days, they had traveled forty-three thousand miles. During that time, Monsignor Sheen delivered more than two hundred speeches, lectures and sermons.

Like the saint whose philosophy and theology he admired and taught, Thomas Aquinas, Archbishop Sheen mixed holiness with brilliance. This piety began early. When he was confirmed at age twelve, he dedicated himself to the Blessed Virgin, to whom he continued devotion throughout his life. He traveled to Lourdes, France thirty times to pray at the site where Mary appeared to Saint Bernadette.

During his TV program, Bishop Sheen would write at the top of his blackboard "JMJ," which viewers soon learned stood for "Jesus, Mary, Joseph." He wrote "JMJ" at the top of everything he wrote, a habit formed when he was in grammar school.

Perhaps, though, the most widely known fact about Bishop Sheen's piety is that he began every day with a Holy Hour in the chapel before the Eucharist. It was a practice he began during his seminary days.

Thomas C. Reeves' book *America's Bishop: The Life and Times of Fulton J. Sheen* reports on Bishop Sheen's special relationship with Rosemont College in Philadelphia. He preached and conducted retreats there frequently. He handed out diplomas at the Catholic women's college in 1955 and, Reeves wrote, "He interrupted the ceremony by announcing the marriage, the next day, of a graduate, calling the young man to the stage and giving an impromptu sermon on Christian marriage." My wife Marie was that graduate and I was the "young man."

The book, however, fails to add that, after I was called to the stage, the other women in the graduating class who were engaged informed Bishop Sheen of their engagement when he handed them their diplomas. He called their fiancés to the stage, too. Nor does the book say that, about ten years later when I was talking with Bishop Sheen at a U.S. bishops' meeting, he told me that the next year he announced that he would be glad to meet with the graduates and their fiancés—after the ceremony.

Bishop Sheen suffered through some trials later in his life. He "retired" from television in 1957, but it seems certain that Cardinal Spellman forced him off the air. The cardinal and the bishop had a falling out when Bishop Sheen refused to spend some of the money of the Society for the Propagation of the Faith as the cardinal wished.

In 1966 Cardinal Spellman got Pope Paul VI to appoint Bishop Sheen the Bishop of Rochester, New York. He had an unsuccessful thirty-four months there, trying to implement the changes of the Second Vatican Council against considerable opposition. Later, in explaining his failure there to Mike Wallace on *60 Minutes*, Bishop Sheen said, "I was never given a chance to administer a diocese before. I am a man of ideas."

He was seventy-four when he left Rochester. He spent the next ten years traveling extensively, preaching and giving retreats, even making some television programs. Then his health began to fade. He underwent open-heart surgery and had prostate surgery. His weight fell to about a hundred twenty-five pounds.

Early in 1979, he agreed to speak at the National Prayer Breakfast, against the advice of his cardiologist. (Billy Graham was asked to be ready to step in if the Archbishop was unable to go on.) Archbishop Sheen got everybody's attention when he turned toward President Jimmy Carter and said, "Mr. President, you are a sinner!" After a suitable pause, he pointed to himself and said, "I am a sinner." After another pause, he looked around the ballroom and said, "We are all sinners, and we all need to turn to God."

Billy Graham later wrote, "He then went on to preach one of the most challenging and eloquent sermons I have ever heard."

When Pope John Paul II visited St. Patrick's Cathedral in New York in October of 1979, a feeble Archbishop Sheen was led to the pope. Archbishop Sheen fell to his knees. The pope helped him to his feet and the two warmly embraced, amid thundering applause. When asked later what the pope had said to him, Archbishop Sheen said, "He told me that I had written and spoken well of the Lord Jesus, and that I was a loyal son of the Church."

Archbishop Sheen had said that he hoped he

would die on one of the Blessed Virgin's feast days. He almost got his wish. He died at age eighty-four on December 9, 1979, the day after the feast of the Immaculate Conception. His body was found in his chapel, before the Blessed Sacrament.

After his death, Archbishop Sheen was buried in St. Patrick's Cathedral, where he had preached so often. Cardinal Terence Cooke explained the reason for his decision to have him buried there when he said that Archbishop John Hughes built the cathedral and Archbishop Sheen filled it.

Under the auspices of Bishop Daniel R. Jenky, C.S.C., Bishop of Peoria, Illinois where Sheen grew up, his cause for beatification was formally opened in the Offices of the Vatican Congregation for the Causes of Saints on April 15, 2008.

CHAPTER THIRTY-SEVEN

PATRICK PEYTON

Father Patrick Peyton is "the Rosary priest" who coined the expression "The family that prays together stays together." Father Theodore Hesburgh, a fellow priest of the Congregation of the Holy Cross and former president of the University of Notre Dame, wrote about Father Peyton, "[He] was one of the most extraordinary priests I have ever known. He always seemed to accomplish what he set out to do, no matter how difficult or visionary it was."

Patrick Peyton grew up in County Mayo, Ireland, where he was born in 1909. He was one of nine children and the family lived in a thatched three-room cabin. What Pat remembered most of his childhood was that the family never failed to gather every evening to recite the Rosary together.

Life was hard for the Peytons and Pat left school to go to work when he was fifteen. His three older sisters moved to the United States where three of his uncles and three of his aunts had gone earlier. When he was nineteen, Pat and his older brother Tom followed them and moved in with an older sister in Scranton, Pennsylvania.

He managed to get a job as sexton (janitor) at the cathedral. He felt a great joy while working there and soon he experienced a desire to be a priest. When he summoned up the courage to tell Monsignor Paul Kelly that he wanted to be a priest, the monsignor's reply surprised Pat: "What's a noun?" he asked. "What's a verb?" Monsignor Kelly was already aware of Pat's vocation but also knew that his education was lacking.

Tom decided that he, too, would test a vocation to the priesthood, so both young men went back to high school with thirteen- and fourteen-year-olds. Monsignor Kelly paid their tuition.

In 1929, some Holy Cross priests from Notre Dame preached a mission at the cathedral. Listening to them, Pat decided that he, too, would like to be a missionary, so he told one of the priests, Father Pat Dolan, that he'd like to join Holy Cross. Tom once again joined his younger brother, and both arrived at Notre Dame in September 1929. First, though, they had to finish three more years of high school. Once they did that, they entered the Holy Cross novitiate and, a year later, began their four-year course at the University of Notre Dame. They graduated *magna cum laude*, twenty-ninth and thirtieth in their class of four hundred sixty-nine. Also, with the statue of Mary at the top of the Golden Dome and the replica of the grotto of Lourdes on campus, Pat increased his already strong devotion to the Blessed Virgin.

After he received his bachelor's degree from Notre Dame, Patrick went to Washington to continue to prepare for the priesthood. But his life changed in October 1938 when he began to cough up blood. He knew that tuberculosis was common in Ireland, but he continued in a state of denial until February 6, 1939. That night he had a violent hemorrhage, blood seeming to pour through his lungs. The doctor who was summoned didn't expect him to survive, but he did, and the next day he was taken by ambulance to Providence Hospital. He lay flat on his back for three months and then was transferred to the infirmary at Notre Dame. Doctors there continued treatment but eventually had to tell Patrick that it was unsuccessful.

Patrick always credited Father Cornelius Hagerty, who taught him philosophy at Notre Dame, for convincing him that he had to have faith in the Blessed Virgin. Father Hagerty told him, "Mary can do anything God can do. The difference is in the way they do it. God wills something and it happens. Mary prays to him for something and he does it. He will never say no to her."

Patrick prayed to Mary to cure him. During his next examination, the doctors noticed definite improvement and a week later they pronounced him cured. Nevertheless, they insisted that he wait for six months to make sure. They did agree, though, that he could return to Washington and resume studies.

He arrived back in Washington, at Holy Cross College, on February 5, 1940, a year after he went to the hospital. He still had to spend most of the day in bed, but a fellow seminarian became his tutor. It was Ted Hesburgh, eight years younger than Peyton. Hesburgh would attend classes and then go to Peyton's room and give him the gist of the lectures. Hesburgh later said, "Pat had a memory like no one else I have ever known. It only took one pass through the morning's lectures and he had it all, not just for then, but for life."

On June 15, 1941, Bishop John Noll of Fort Wayne ordained Patrick, now thirty-two, and his brother Tom at Notre Dame. However, since he had missed a year of schooling, Patrick had to return to Holy Cross to complete his studies.

Father Peyton had already determined to

devote the rest of his life to promoting devotion to Mary. In 1942 he showed Ted Hesburgh, who would be ordained in 1943, a letter to Bishop Edwin O'Hara of Kansas City, who had recently spoken to the seminarians about the Confraternity of Christian Doctrine that he had helped establish. Father Peyton asked Hesburgh to edit the letter and type it for him, which he did. The letter asked the bishop to approve and promote Father Peyton's idea for what he called "The Family Rosary." Bishop O'Hara replied enthusiastically, and that was the beginning of what became a worldwide crusade.

Father Peyton, with the permission of his religious superior, began to spread the word and ask for help. He went to Bishop (later Cardinal) John O'Hara, who had been president of the University of Notre Dame and was then head of military chaplains. He ordered all chaplains to preach on the family Rosary. He got Holy Cross Father Charles Sheedy (later dean of Notre Dame's College of Arts and Letters) to write an article about the Family Rosary Crusade for the national Catholic weekly *Our Sunday Visitor*. He made the rounds in Washington and got promises of financial support from the National Council of Catholic Men, the National Council of Catholic Women, the Catholic Daughters of America, the Legion of Mary, the Knights of Columbus, and other Catholic organizations. The Knights made promotion of the family Rosary one of their objectives.

Monsignor Fulton J. Sheen agreed to announce on his *Catholic Hour* radio program that he would send copies of the pamphlet *The Story of the Family Rosary* and Rosary beads to any listener who wrote in. There were fifty thousand requests!

Realizing the power of radio at that time, Father Peyton decided to take advantage of it. He had been saying the Rosary over a station in Albany, New York, but he wanted to go national. He convinced the Mutual network to give him airtime free of charge on Mother's Day of 1945. World War II was just ending and he got the parents of the five Sullivans who had been killed during that war to pray the Rosary. Archbishop Spellman of New York participated. And Father Peyton got on the telephone, managed to contact Bing Crosby in Hollywood, and convinced him to be part of the program. It was a resounding success.

Father Peyton was then encouraged to go to Hollywood to get other stars to help him with his radio apostolate. It wasn't long before he convinced about thirty stars (eventually more than a hundred) to contribute their services on any free time he could get on radio networks. They included Bing Crosby, Loretta Young, Irene Dunn, Pat O'Brien, Maureen O'Sullivan, Jane Wyatt, Gregory Peck, Ethel Barrymore, Shirley Temple, Jimmy Durante, and many more.

Tom Lewis, Loretta Young's husband who worked for Young and Rubikam, put together a team of script writers and *The Family Theater of the Air* was broadcast over the Mutual network for the first time on February 13, 1947. The stars of the first broadcast, a drama called "Flight from Home," were Loretta Young, Jimmy Stewart and Don Ameche. The commercials tried to sell the idea of family prayer. Soon the show's slogan "The family that prays together stays together" was well known throughout the country.

The Family Theater of the Air had a successful ten-year run on radio during the 1940s and 1950s. At its peak four hundred twenty-nine stations carried it and Father Peyton was in constant motion raising the money for its production. It won numerous awards. But by the mid-1950s, television was becoming more important, and Father Peyton turned his attention to that new medium.

He began by developing an hour-long Christmas show called *The Joyful Hour*. That was followed by *The Triumphant Hour* at Easter, both carried on the Mutual network. The response was so good that Mutual contributed time for special programs for Mother's Day and Thanksgiving. All except the Thanksgiving program included the praying of the Rosary, led by Hollywood stars. Perry Como sang the Ave Maria.

All the time Father Peyton was working on these shows, and raising money to produce them, he was also preaching triduums (three-day missions) about the family Rosary. This led to the diocesan Family Rosary Crusade. The crusade began in Canada and then spread to Scranton, Baltimore, Washington, and throughout the country.

Parishes in the dioceses recruited men to visit each home in the parish to solicit pledges to pray the family Rosary. Father Peyton (probably somewhat of a chauvinist) preferred that men, rather than women, be recruited because he believed that if men were involved the family Rosary would be more likely to be prayed. During the 1950s families throughout the country were praying the family Rosary. After families signed up, Father Peyton would speak at diocesan rallies, which attracted large crowds.

Father Peyton then turned his attention overseas. He had successful Rosary crusades in several dioceses in England. Bishop (later Cardinal) Angel Herrera of Malaga, Spain happened to be in London while the crusade was being organized, and asked Father Peyton to go to Spain. He did, and he took a crash course in the Spanish language in Malaga.

After his crusade in Malaga, Father Peyton had requests from bishops around the world. He eventually led crusades and spoke at rallies in Australia, New Zealand, and then in his native land of Ireland. From there the next stop was Latin America. It was there that the Family Rosary Crusade achieved its greatest success. He began in Chile, then in Venezuela, Colombia, Brazil, the Dominican Republic, Panama, and Ecuador. His rallies brought out two hundred fifty thousand in Panama City, six hundred thousand in Caracas, Venezuela; a million in Bogota, Colombia; a million and a half in Rio de Janeiro, Brazil; and two million in São Paulo, Brazil.

The Family Rosary Crusade circled the globe. Father Peyton preached in thirty-three Indian dioceses and in thirteen dioceses of Burma, Malaya, Thailand, Ceylon and Pakistan. In Africa he preached in dioceses in Kenya, Tanganyika, Uganda and South Africa.

He was still preaching Rosary Crusades as late as 1985 when his rally in the Philippines attracted two million people. But well before that he also turned his attention to movies. While he was studying Spanish in Malaga, Spain, he got the idea of producing a series of fifteen half-hour movies, one for each of the (then) mysteries of the Rosary. As always, his first problem was to raise the money to produce them. But, typically for Father Peyton, he was able to coax and cajole the money needed—a million dollars.

He decided to film the movies in Spain. It was cheaper to do it there, Madrid had excellent studio facilities, the scenery was close to that of the Holy Land, and it was easy to find extras with facial characteristics similar to those of Palestine. The movies were filmed in Spanish and then other languages dubbed. Filming began in 1955 and was completed in 1957. The first showing was at the Vatican Pavilion at the World's Fair in Brussels, Belgium, in 1957.

The films changed the nature of the Rosary Rallies, especially in Latin America. Two of the films were shown each evening for a week in stadiums or big public squares. Speakers spoke briefly at the end of each mystery. On the eighth day, with one film remaining, a Mass or recitation of the Rosary followed.

The films were also shown in hospitals, barracks and prisons. More than twenty million people attended the rallies and viewed the films as part of the diocesan Rosary Crusade in countries throughout Latin America. Parish campaigns to get families to pledge to recite the family Rosary followed the rallies.

During the 1960s Father Peyton concentrated on Latin America, but he also had large rallies in other parts of the world: in San Francisco and Sacramento, in nine dioceses of the Philippines, and in several dioceses in Spain.

Meanwhile, in the United States, he continued to raise funds to produce other films for television. One was *The World's Greatest Mother*, depicting important events in the life of Mary. Another was *Trial at Tara*, the story of Saint Patrick. Still another was an adaptation of Francis Thompson's poem *Hound of Heaven*. In all, he produced fourteen more TV programs, including two three-part series on the Rosary, one featuring Princess Grace of Monaco and another Loretta Young. He also continued to conduct Rosary crusades.

By the time he died on June 3, 1992 at age eighty-three, Father Peyton had conducted Rosary crusades in forty countries, attracting twenty-eight million people. He produced more than six hundred radio and TV dramas that were broadcast ten thousand times. Not bad for an immigrant boy who came to the United States to escape a life of poverty in Ireland and made it his life's work to promote family prayer and the Rosary.

On October 7, 1995, Pope John Paul II gave a talk on family prayer and then led the Rosary at St. Patrick's Cathedral in New York City. During his talk, he said, "To use a phrase made famous by the late Father Patrick Peyton, 'The family that prays together stays together.'"

CHAPTER THIRTY-EIGHT

WALTER CISZEK

When Walter Ciszek, born in 1904, was growing up in Shenandoah, Pennsylvania, he seemed an unlikely candidate for the priesthood. He later wrote in his autobiography that he was "tough, stubborn, a bully, the leader of a gang, a street fighter." So his father was amazed when Walter announced, after he completed eighth grade, that he wanted to be a priest.

His parents had immigrated to the United States from Poland and his father had gotten a job as a coal miner. Later he owned a saloon. The couple had thirteen children. Walter was their seventh child and he was a problem for his parents. He skipped school so often that he had to repeat a grade at St. Casimir's Grade School. His father became so frustrated with his son that he begged the police to send him to reform school. Is it any wonder that he was surprised when Walter said that he wanted to be a priest?

He entered Saints Cyril and Methodius Seminary at Orchard Lake, Michigan. He kept in top physical condition by running five miles a day and swimming in a cold lake. He disciplined his body one Lent by eating nothing except bread and water, and he gave up meat during another Lent. He said that he always wanted to do "the hardest thing," so he gave up playing baseball, a sport he loved, just to prove that he could do it.

When a priest talked about the toughness of the Jesuit Saint Stanislaus Kostka, who had walked from Warsaw to Rome when he decided to be a priest, Walter decided that he too wanted to be a Jesuit. He enrolled at St. Andrew's Novitiate in Poughkeepsie, New York. He studied at the Jesuit seminaries at Wernersville, Pennsylvania and Woodstock, Maryland before finishing his education at Gregorian University and the Russian College in Rome. He was ordained in the Basilica of St. Paul Outside the Walls on June 24, 1937.

Well before his ordination—while he was still in the novitiate, in fact—he became enthusiastic about going to the Soviet Union. Pope Pius XI had sent a letter "to all seminarians, especially our Jesuit sons," in which he sought volunteers to serve the communist-persecuted Church in the Soviet Union. Walter had, therefore, studied everything he could get his hands on about the

Soviet Union—its geography, history, language, culture, and its eastern rite. After his ordination, therefore, his Jesuit superior assigned him to a parish in Albertyn, Poland, where he waited for a chance to minister in Russia.

It took two years, but Father Ciszek and a friend saw their chance when Germany and the Soviet Union invaded Poland in September of 1939. They managed to get false permits that would allow them to work in the Ural Mountains. Then they hopped a railroad boxcar headed for Russia. Using the alias Vladimir Lypinski, Father Ciszek got a job hauling logs from a river and piling them on shore. He and his friend celebrated Mass on a tree stump, taking turns standing guard while the other said Mass. Gradually, believers learned of the priests' presence and Father Ciszek and his friends gave them instructions at night.

In 1941, after Germany invaded the Soviet Union, the KGB arrested Father Ciszek and hundreds of others. He was surprised to learn that the KGB knew his real name, his national origin, and the fact that he was a priest. However, they thought he was a German spy. They sent him to the infamous Lubjanka Prison in Moscow. For four years, he was confined to a cell measuring six by ten feet, with nothing in it except a bed and a bucket that served as a toilet. Guards watched constantly. He was allowed out of the cell for twenty minutes daily for exercise. He spent his time praying the Mass prayers, the Angelus, several rosaries, and other prayers.

He also underwent "relentless questioning." When he tried to explain that all he was doing was "priestly work," his interrogators couldn't understand that and were convinced that he must have had some other reason for being there. Eventually, after being given drug-laced tea, he confessed to being a Vatican spy. When presented with an agreement to work as a spy for the Soviet Union, he refused, and was beaten.

He was sentenced to fifteen years of hard labor, the first four at Lubjanka and Butirka prisons. Then he was sent to Siberia where he spent eleven years at two slave-labor camps, Dudinka and Norilsk. He was forced to work as a coal miner, log-retriever, and construction worker. In those camps, though, he was also able to work as a priest among his fellow prisoners. He said Mass for the first time in five years while at Dudinka, and at Norilsk he was imprisoned with a dozen priests from the Baltic and Poland.

Meanwhile, no one in the United States or in Poland had heard from him since his arrest in 1941. His Jesuit community declared him officially dead in 1947 and had Masses said for him.

In 1955, three months before the end of his fifteen-year sentence, he was released, but told to remain in Norilsk, Siberia. He moved into a small apartment where he lived with two other priests. He and the other priests celebrated Mass, performed baptisms and weddings, and visited the sick. The priests were being watched closely, though, and he was repeatedly warned not to engage in "subversive activities." He replied that he was doing nothing other than praying for the people who came to him.

In 1958, the Soviet government ordered him to leave Norilsk. He did so, traveling some seven hundred miles south to the town of Krasnoyarsk, where another priest had suddenly "disappeared." When he began to minister there, the government sent him to nearby Abakan.

Then in 1963, the KGB summoned Father Ciszek to its offices and took him to Moscow. On October 11 of that year, he and another American were exchanged for a Russian couple who had been convicted of spying in the United States. He was put on a plane for the United States. He was then fifty-nine years old and had been out of the United States for twenty-eight years, since he left to study in Rome.

The Jesuits assigned him to the John XXIII Center for Eastern Studies at Fordham University, where he taught and gave retreats. He also wrote two books: his autobiography, *With God in Russia*, published in 1964, and *He Leadeth Me*, a spiritual journal, published in 1973. In his autobiography he wrote that he survived his years in Russia because of God's providence. He wrote, "God has a special purpose, a special love, a special providence for all those he has created. God cares for each of us individually, watches over us, provides for us."

Father Ciszek died at Fordham on the feast of the Immaculate Conception, December 8, 1984, at age eighty.

CHAPTER THIRTY-NINE

TERENCE COOKE

Contrary to what you might expect, it's unusual for a bishop, archbishop or cardinal to be considered for sainthood. Only one canonized American saint was a bishop—John Neumann—although three others are being considered—Frederic Baraga, Simon Bruté and Fulton J. Sheen.

So Terence J. Cooke, the cardinal-archbishop of New York, really stood out for his sanctity. He became Archbishop of New York in 1968 and a cardinal in 1969.

Cardinal Cooke was always a New Yorker. He was born in 1921, the third child of Irish immigrants in Morningside Heights in Upper Manhattan. His parents, Michael and Margaret Gannon Cooke, named him in honor of Terence MacSwiney, who had recently died in a hunger strike while protesting the British occupation of Ireland.

It was a devout family. His parents taught him the importance of daily prayer, the Eucharist, and devotion to the Blessed Virgin. But when he was nine, his mother died. Her single sister Mary moved into the home to care for the children.

From his earliest days, Terence wanted to be a priest. He entered the archdiocesan seminary after finishing the eighth grade at St. Benedict's Elementary School. He attended Cathedral College and then St. Joseph's Seminary at Dunwoodie. Cardinal Francis Spellman ordained him a priest in St. Patrick's Cathedral on December 1, 1945.

After his ordination, he was sent to the University of Chicago to obtain a graduate degree in social work. He was there only two weeks, though, before he was forced to withdraw because of an eye ailment that he had had for some time. That cleared up sufficiently a couple years later and he was able to enroll at the National Catholic School of Social Service at the Catholic University of America in Washington, D.C. He received a master's degree there in 1949.

After returning to New York, his advancement in the bureaucracy of the Church was meteoric. He began in the Youth Division of Catholic Charities for five years before being named procurator of St. Joseph's Seminary. In 1957 he was appointed secretary to Cardinal Francis Spellman. A year later he was named vice chancellor of the archdiocese. He became chancellor in 1961 and vicar general and auxiliary bishop in 1965. He became archbishop after Cardinal Spellman's death, probably on the cardinal's recommendation. He was only forty-six, the youngest of the archdiocese's ten auxiliary bishops. He also succeeded Cardinal Spellman as military vicar for the Armed Forces.

He was a very different archbishop from his predecessor, known as a holy and extremely kind man. He listened attentively and worked quietly but diligently.

Unbeknown to the public, Cardinal Cooke was diagnosed with cancer in 1964, when he was only forty-three. He had been treated with chemotherapy and blood transfusions, which only a few people knew about. He never reduced his workload. In 1975 he was told that the cancer had spread to a terminal condition. He still did not reduce his workload.

It wasn't until August of 1983 that the public learned about the cancer. He could no longer work as he had been doing and doctors told him that his time was short.

He died on October 6, 1983, when he was sixty-two. His last letter to the people of the archdiocese was read in churches on October 9, which happened to be Pro-Life Sunday. He wrote, in part: "At this grace-filled time of my life, as I experience suffering in union with Jesus Our Lord and Redeemer, I offer gratitude to Almighty God for giving me the opportunity to continue my apostolate on behalf of life."

Cardinal Cooke always saw himself as a simple priest. In their book *Thy Will Be Done: A Spiritual Portrait of Terence Cardinal Cooke* (ST PAULS / Alba House), Father Benedict Groeschel and Terrence L. Weber include a quotation from Cardinal Cooke, taken from handwritten notes, that the authors say sums up how the cardinal "saw himself and his vocation as a priest." Cardinal Cooke wrote:

> From the day of his ordination, a priest can never forget that he has been called by God himself. The priest is called to be a *servant*, giving up a family of his own, so that he can minister to those who need him more. The priest is called to be a *victim*, ready to share the sufferings of his people and not hide from them, and even ready to bear their sufferings in their place if God asks him to do so. A priest is called to be a *brother*, who shares the worries and fears and

the frailty of the people around him, and who brings to them not any great strength and invulnerability of his own, but his joyful trust in the Father who loves him in Jesus whose priesthood he shares. The priest is called to be a *listener,* to learn prayerfully from the way in which God has worked in the lives of His people, and full of faith to carry that message to others. A priest is called to be a *friend,* conscious of the need of justice and brotherly concern in our society, a friend to people who have few friends in their hour of need. The anointing that Jesus gives us is to help us bring Him into our world, not to carry us out of it.

CHAPTER FORTY

VINCENT CAPODANNO

Vincent Capodanno was born on February 13, 1929 in Staten Island, New York. After his ordination, he worked as a missionary in Taiwan and Hong Kong before serving in the Marines as a United States Navy Chaplain.

In 1966, "Fr. Vince" was sent to Vietnam. According to CatholicMil.Org, "He gained a reputation for always being there—for always taking care of his Marines."

On September 4, 1967, Chaplain Capodanno received word of a battle taking place, Operation Swift. He knew that it wouldn't be easy, and that the fighting was fierce, but he went among the wounded and dying, to give last rites to his Marines. Though blasts wounded his face and hands, "Father Capodanno moved to help a wounded corpsman only yards from an enemy machine gun. Father Capodanno died taking care of one of his men."

Fr. Capodanno was posthumously awarded the Medal of Honor in recognition of his selfless sacrifice and was given the title "Servant of God" on May 21, 2006, thirty-nine years after his death on the battlefield of Vietnam.

The memorial Mass marking the 41st anniversary of his death is being requested by CatholicMil.Org, which is also the petitioner for his cause of Sainthood.

ACKNOWLEDGMENTS AND BIBLIOGRAPHY

My primary source for this book was *Saints of North America*, by Vincent J. O'Malley, C.M., published in 2004 by Our Sunday Visitor Publishing Division. Fortunately for me, Father O'Malley included not only canonized saints but also official candidates for sainthood—servants of God, venerables, and blesseds.

Besides Father O'Malley's book, I offer the following bibliography:

Portraits of American Sanctity, by Joseph N. Tylenda, Franciscan Herald Press, 1982.

Our American Catholic Heritage, by Albert J. Nevins, M.M., Our Sunday Visitor, Huntington, IN, 1972.

The Encyclopedia of American Catholic History, A Michael Glazier Book, Collegeville, MN, 1997.

Faces of Holiness: Modern Saints in Photos and Words, by Ann Ball, Our Sunday Visitor, 1998.

Patriotic Leaders of the Church, by John F. Fink, Our Sunday Visitor, 2004 (for Isaac Hecker and Fulton J. Sheen).

American Martyrs from 1542, by Albert J. Nevins, M.N., Our Sunday Visitor, 1987.

Giant in the Wilderness: A Biography of Father Charles Nerinckx, by Helene Magaret, The Bruce Publishing Co., 1952.

The Memoirs of Father Samuel Mazzuchelli, O.P., by Samuel Mazzuchelli, The Priory Press, 1967.

Henriette Delille: "Servant of Slaves," by Virginia Meacham Gould and Charles E. Nolan, Sisters of the Holy Family, New Orleans, 1999.

Response to Love: The Story of Mother Mary Elizabeth Lange, O.S.P., by Maria M. Lannon, Josephite Pastoral Center, Washington, DC, 1992.

Parish Priest: Father Michael McGivney and American Catholicism, by Douglas Brinkley and Julie M. Fenster, William Morrow, an imprint of HarperCollins, 2006.

The Yankee Paul: Isaac Hecker, by Vincent F. Holden, Bruce Publishing Co., 1958.

As God Shall Ordain: A History of the Franciscan Sisters of Chicago, 1894-1987, by Anne Marie Knawa, O.S.F., Worzalla Publishing Co., Lemont, Ill., 1989.

Servant of God, Monsignor Nelson H. Baker (1841-1936), One Lifetime, by Boniface Hanley, O.F.M., St. Anthony Guild, Paterson, NJ, no date.

Out of Many Hearts: Mother M. Alphonsa Lathrop and Her Work, by Mary Joseph Blessington, O.P., The Servants of Relief for Incurable Cancer, Hawthorne, NY, 1965.

Acknowledgments and Bibliography

"The More Things Change, the More They Are the Same" (Life of Rose Hawthorne Lathrop), by Boniface Hanley, O.F.M., St. Anthony Guild, Paterson, NJ, 1985.

The Founders of Maryknoll: Historical Reflections, by Robert E. Sheridan, M.M., Catholic Foreign Mission Society of America, Inc., Maryknoll, N.Y., 1980.

Greater Perfection Conferences, by Miriam Teresa Demjanovich, edited by Charles C. Demjanovich, Paterson, NJ, 1983.

Solanus Casey: The Official Account of a Virtuous American Life, edited by Michael Crosby, O.F.M. Cap., The Crossroad Publishing Co., 2000.

The Long Loneliness: An Autobiography, by Dorothy Day, Harper San Francisco, 1952.

The Servant of God Mother M. Angeline Teresa, O. Carm. (1893-1984), Daughter of Carmel, Mother to the Aged, by Jude Mead, C.P., St. Bede's Publication, Petersham, MA, 1990.

Fragments of My Life, by Catherine de Hueck Doherty, Madonna House Publications, Combermere, Ont., Canada, 1996.

They Called Her the Baroness: The Life of Catherine de Hueck Doherty, by Lorene Hanley Duquin, Alba House, Staten Island, NY, 1995.

America's Bishop: The Life and Times of Fulton J. Sheen, by Thomas C. Reeves, Encounter Books, San Francisco, 2001.

Treasure in Clay: The Autobiography of Fulton J. Sheen, Doubleday, New York, 1980.

All for Her: The Autobiography of Father Patrick Peyton, C.S.C., Doubleday, 1967.

With God in Russia, by Walter Ciszek, The America Press, New York, 1964.

Thy Will Be Done: A Spiritual Portrait of Terence Cardinal Cooke, by Benedict J. Groeschel, C.F.R., and Terrence L. Weber, Alba House, 1990.